Library of
Davidson College

Cover and book design: Pat Taylor

Appendix B (continued)

Standard Industrial Classification	Advertising-to-Sales Ratio (in percents)	Concentration Ratio (in percents)	Standard Industrial Classification	Advertising-to-Sales Ratio (in percents)	Concentration Ratio (in percents)
3576	0.68	53	3715	0.47	48
3579	2.01	63	3721	0.11	69
3581	0.93	60	3722	0.12	64
3582	0.79	51	3731	0.08	42
3586	0.85	56	3741	0.28	97
3589	0.74	14	3742	0.22	53
3611	0.31	35	3791	0.15	19
3612	0.24	65	3799	0.44	15
3623	0.23	38	3811	1.59	28
3629	0.24	30	3821	1.79	20
3636	9.54	81	3831	0.34	49
3661	0.30	92	3841	3.02	38
3662	0.22	22	3843	3.17	41
3693	0.31	62			
3713	2.04	21	Sample size = 53		

Appendix B (continued)

Standard Industrial Classification	Advertising-to-Sales Ratio (in percents)	Concentration Ratio (in percents)	Standard Industrial Classification	Advertising-to-Sales Ratio (in percents)	Concentration Ratio (in percents)
3425	0.86	51	3861	1.57	69
3429	0.51	38	3872	3.81	68
3431	1.71	51	3912	1.80	31
3432	0.96	28	3952	4.20	42
3433	1.49	22	3953	2.49	30
3441	0.43	13	3955	1.33	37
3442	0.50	10	3962	0.25	19
3443	0.31	30	3963	0.87	26
3444	0.44	10	3964	0.61	47
3446	0.38	28	3991	3.16	33
3449	0.38	21	3993	2.21	6
3461	0.33	39	3994	2.80	22
3471	0.20	5	3999	1.97	10
3479	0.15	18			
3481	0.31	11	Sample size = 184		
3491	0.56	36			
3493	0.26	27	*Producer Durables*		
3496	0.31	61	2521	2.10	29
3497	2.94	43	2522	2.29	38
3499	0.22	14	2531	0.14	23
3519	0.38	47	2541	0.41	6
3534	2.11	55	2542	0.14	24
3536	0.43	44	2599	0.17	18
3561	0.64	26	3511	0.51	88
3562	0.56	54	3522	1.46	44
3564	0.64	23	3531	0.38	41
3565	0.44	9	3532	0.54	37
3566	0.39	25	3533	0.59	21
3585	0.85	31	3535	0.65	29
3599	0.47	7	3537	0.79	48
3613	0.52	51	3541	0.40	21
3621	0.20	48	3542	0.47	23
3622	0.21	49	3548	0.58	26
3624	0.23	86	3551	0.55	22
3641	2.48	91	3552	0.42	31
3642	1.32	19	3553	0.53	37
3674	0.74	47	3554	0.50	43
3679	0.68	32	3555	0.41	48
3691	0.38	61	3559	0.36	13
3694	0.51	66	3567	0.54	36
3699	0.21	23	3569	0.53	10
3822	2.20	56	3572	1.06	81
3842	4.01	44			

Appendix B (continued)

Standard Industrial Classification	Advertising-to-Sales Ratio (in percents)	Concentration Ratio (in percents)	Standard Industrial Classification	Advertising-to-Sales Ratio (in percents)	Concentration Ratio (in percents)
2642	0.56	32	3241	0.35	29
2643	0.77	23	3251	0.42	14
2644	3.33	39	3253	1.68	52
2645	0.77	37	3255	0.33	44
2646	0.75	71	3259	0.34	31
2649	0.78	29	3261	2.10	62
2661	0.73	46	3262	2.36	70
2711	0.48	16	3264	0.22	47
2721	2.24	24	3269	0.78	28
2732	1.79	21	3271	0.33	4
2741	0.47	29	3272	0.37	11
2753	0.88	21	3273	0.37	6
2761	0.31	47	3274	0.28	35
2782	0.29	35	3275	0.70	80
2789	0.65	11	3281	0.87	18
2791	0.64	7	3291	1.29	48
2793	0.73	10	3292	0.65	55
2794	1.49	34	3293	0.73	30
2821	1.62	27	3295	0.34	26
2822	1.14	61	3296	0.47	71
2823	1.17	86	3297	0.33	38
2824	1.70	84	3299	0.51	37
2843	10.57	34	3312	0.27	48
2851	2.00	22	3313	0.30	74
2861	2.28	70	3315	0.29	24
2871	1.23	35	3316	0.28	34
2872	0.68	23	3317	0.29	32
2879	1.74	39	3331	0.22	77
2891	2.50	27	3333	0.29	59
2892	2.46	67	3339	0.23	60
2893	2.55	49	3341	0.30	26
2895	2.41	72	3351	0.21	41
2899	2.51	19	3352	0.75	65
2951	0.18	14	3356	0.22	49
2952	0.22	38	3357	0.34	39
3011	2.92	70	3361	0.46	24
3031	1.86	87	3362	0.27	18
3069	1.60	21	3369	0.22	29
3079	0.72	8	3391	0.20	30
3111	0.11	20	3392	0.15	77
3121	0.40	62	3399	0.16	14
3131	0.50	19	3411	1.00	73
3221	0.43	60	3423	0.69	22

Appendix B (continued)

Standard Industrial Classification	Advertising-to-Sales Ratio (in percents)	Concentration Ratio (in percents)	Standard Industrial Classification	Advertising-to-Sales Ratio (in percents)	Concentration Ratio (in percents)
3199	1.89	19	*Producer Nondurables*		
3692	1.26	85	2041	1.54	30
3941	5.79	25	2042	1.85	23
3942	5.85	19	2046	0.21	68
			2083	1.20	39
Sample size = 54			2087	1.10	67
			2091	0.30	42
			2092	1.01	55
Consumer Durables			2093	0.30	56
2391	1.14	27	2094	0.33	28
2392	1.02	21	2097	0.52	33
2511	1.03	12	2141	0.10	63
2512	1.00	14	2241	0.60	19
2514	0.98	14	2256	0.38	15
2515	1.15	26	2284	0.70	62
2519	11.19	36	2291	1.02	61
2591	1.04	41	2292	0.48	31
2731	2.24	20	2293	1.06	34
3161	1.65	34	2294	0.12	36
3263	1.91	61	2295	0.16	31
3421	15.06	69	2296	0.16	83
3631	4.01	56	2297	0.07	61
3632	3.07	73	2298	0.96	34
3633	4.97	78	2299	1.83	37
3634	10.06	52	2393	0.07	31
3635	3.67	76	2394	0.15	20
3639	3.29	44	2395	0.14	7
3651	3.74	49	2396	0.09	57
3652	4.59	58	2397	0.10	13
3732	1.31	19	2399	0.08	19
3751	2.68	57	2411	0.04	14
3851	2.76	51	2421	0.25	11
3871	3.03	47	2426	0.60	15
3911	1.06	23	2429	0.35	21
3913	0.47	30	2431	0.51	9
3914	2.72	56	2432	0.56	26
3931	2.42	35	2433	0.43	21
3943	5.45	57	2491	0.09	35
3949	2.10	28	2499	1.08	15
3951	2.70	46	2611	0.12	45
3961	2.72	22	2621	0.50	26
3996	3.66	89	2631	0.49	27
Sample size = 33			2641	0.63	38

Appendix B (continued)

Standard Industrial Classification	Advertising-to-Sales Ratio (in percents)	Concentration Ratio (in percents)	Standard Industrial Classification	Advertising-to-Sales Ratio (in percents)	Concentration Ratio (in percents)
3561	0.66	26	2026	0.52	22
3567	0.54	28	2031	3.25	44
3569	0.53	22	2032	5.54	69
3571	0.84	67	2033	3.18	22
3572	1.10	76	2034	2.35	32
3576	0.46	50	2035	10.71	33
3579	1.99	59	2036	1.00	26
3581	0.48	55	2037	2.48	24
3582	0.50	47	2043	18.53	88
3586	0.49	46	2044	1.45	46
3589	0.59	14	2045	4.29	68
3611	0.27	34	2051	1.31	26
3612	0.26	68	2052	1.56	59
3661	0.23	92	2071	4.49	25
3662	0.27	29	2072	4.08	77
3693	0.26	67	2073	4.25	86
3713	2.14	22	2082	8.60	40
3715	0.28	59	2084	6.43	48
3721	0.12	59	2085	5.05	54
3722	0.12	57	2086	4.83	13
3729	0.12	38	2095	4.46	53
3731	0.09	48	2096	3.80	43
3741	0.27	97	2098	3.28	31
3742	0.22	53	2099	5.22	24
3799	0.14	14	2111	5.85	81
3811	2.34	29	2121	4.23	59
3831	0.49	41	2131	6.76	51
3841	5.68	47	2251	1.01	32
3843	4.39	37	2252	0.97	25
			2253	0.32	15
			2254	0.07	36
			2259	10.57	54
			2647	0.92	63
			2771	0.34	67
			2841	10.61	70
			2842	10.26	35
			2844	28.77	38
			3021	1.94	59
			3141	1.04	7
			3142	0.58	22
			3151	2.03	30
			3171	1.67	10
			3172	1.84	33

Sample size = 50

1967

Consumer Nondurables

2011	0.29	26
2013	0.33	15
2015	0.30	15
2021	0.41	15
2022	0.86	44
2023	1.99	41
2024	1.39	33

Appendix B (continued)

Standard Industrial Classification	Advertising-to-Sales Ratio (in percents)	Concentration Ratio (in percents)	Standard Industrial Classification	Advertising-to-Sales Ratio (in percents)	Concentration Ratio (in percents)
3423	0.93	21	3692	1.46	89
3425	0.91	48	3694	0.53	69
3429	0.53	39	3699	0.22	38
3431	1.53	49	3821	2.38	22
3432	1.16	30	3822	2.76	55
3433	1.41	16	3842	5.60	49
3441	0.50	15	3861	1.85	63
3442	0.49	8	3872	0.69	57
3443	0.49	25	3912	0.18	33
3444	0.61	11	3952	2.73	37
3446	0.57	13	3953	2.72	40
3449	0.52	25	3955	2.78	38
3461	0.64	13	3962	0.19	17
3471	0.24	5	3963	0.18	27
3479	0.24	17	3964	0.80	34
3481	0.33	13	3981	2.90	31
3491	0.62	40	3993	2.61	5
3493	0.24	44	3999	2.62	13
3496	0.24	58			
3497	3.31	54	Sample size = 189		
3499	0.25	16			
3519	0.48	49	Producer Durables		
3532	0.51	35	2521	2.40	29
3534	2.23	62	2522	2.48	33
3536	0.48	36	2531	0.14	24
3562	0.53	57	2541	0.42	4
3564	0.69	27	2542	0.14	23
3565	0.52	9	2599	0.15	16
3566	0.53	24	3511	0.47	93
3585	0.85	25	3522	1.75	43
3599	0.46	8	3531	0.48	42
3613	0.51	51	3533	0.50	25
3621	0.26	50	3535	0.55	28
3622	0.25	56	3537	0.75	54
3623	0.26	41	3541	0.49	20
3624	0.26	83	3542	0.48	22
3629	0.25	38	3548	0.69	25
3639	3.22	41	3551	0.62	22
3641	2.14	92	3552	0.47	35
3642	1.56	17	3553	0.48	35
3674	0.86	46	3554	0.48	41
3679	1.10	13	3555	0.49	44
3691	0.38	59	3559	0.49	10

Appendix B (continued)

Standard Industrial Classification	Advertising-to-Sales Ratio (in percents)	Concentration Ratio (in percents)	Standard Industrial Classification	Advertising-to-Sales Ratio (in percents)	Concentration Ratio (in percents)
2641	0.27	30	3221	0.59	55
2642	0.65	32	3241	0.36	29
2643	1.39	22	3251	0.46	12
2644	0.70	33	3253	1.54	49
2645	0.76	36	3255	0.31	41
2646	0.62	72	3259	0.32	36
2649	1.25	23	3261	2.21	57
2661	1.26	47	3262	2.71	69
2711	0.50	15	3264	0.38	46
2721	2.45	28	3269	0.81	32
2732	0.09	19	3271	0.33	5
2741	0.57	32	3272	0.46	17
2753	0.80	26	3273	0.42	4
2761	0.17	46	3274	0.31	37
2782	0.74	33	3275	0.60	84
2789	0.64	12	3281	0.88	20
2791	0.65	6	3291	1.34	58
2793	0.64	8	3292	0.74	56
2794	0.67	31	3293	0.78	35
2821	1.84	35	3295	0.39	24
2822	1.17	57	3296	0.54	67
2823	1.20	82	3297	0.37	49
2824	2.01	94	3299	0.45	37
2843	0.55	39	3312	0.28	48
2851	2.10	23	3313	0.24	79
2861	1.23	63	3315	0.24	28
2871	1.02	34	3316	0.24	36
2872	1.21	20	3317	0.24	27
2879	2.00	33	3331	0.22	78
2891	2.45	28	3333	0.30	57
2892	3.68	72	3339	0.28	61
2893	1.65	48	3341	0.33	29
2895	1.63	72	3351	0.30	45
2899	3.90	20	3352	0.96	68
2951	0.24	15	3356	0.29	46
2952	0.21	37	3357	0.52	44
3011	2.49	70	3361	0.50	33
3031	0.24	93	3362	0.29	18
3069	1.46	23	3369	0.29	18
3079	0.64	8	3391	0.24	30
3111	0.13	18	3392	0.24	84
3121	0.15	67	3399	0.24	17
3131	0.52	20	3411	1.05	74

Appendix B (continued)

Standard Industrial Classification	Advertising-to-Sales Ratio (in percents)	Concentration Ratio (in percents)	Standard Industrial Classification	Advertising-to-Sales Ratio (in percents)	Concentration Ratio (in percents)
3984	2.65	38	\multicolumn{3}{l}{*Producer Nondurables*}
3988	2.65	20	2034	2.42	37
\multicolumn{3}{l}{Sample size = 54}	2041	0.97	35
			2042	1.78	22
			2046	0.21	71
\multicolumn{3}{l}{*Consumer Durables*}	2083	0.53	38
2391	1.19	21	2087	1.28	62
2392	1.12	18	2091	0.23	41
2511	1.06	11	2092	1.06	50
2512	1.03	13	2093	0.25	58
2514	1.02	13	2094	0.35	23
2515	1.17	26	2097	0.56	32
2519	21.67	34	2141	0.11	70
2591	0.68	37	2241	0.63	20
2731	4.13	20	2256	0.39	18
3161	1.73	31	2284	0.82	68
3263	1.92	57	2291	1.08	54
3421	17.15	66	2292	0.30	27
3631	3.75	51	2293	1.07	28
3632	2.98	74	2294	0.17	38
3633	4.89	78	2295	0.17	34
3634	9.91	41	2296	0.17	79
3635	3.39	81	2297	0.07	61
3651	4.19	41	2298	1.15	35
3652	3.83	69	2299	2.18	38
3717	0.63	77	2393	0.04	38
3732	1.31	21	2394	0.50	18
3751	2.60	56	2395	0.03	9
3791	0.15	22	2396	0.03	58
3851	3.57	53	2397	0.03	13
3871	3.75	46	2399	0.11	14
3911	3.11	26	2411	0.04	11
3913	0.06	38	2421	0.28	11
3914	3.73	55	2426	0.28	17
3931	2.40	38	2429	0.29	17
3943	0.94	43	2431	0.52	7
3949	2.12	37	2432	0.57	23
3951	2.48	48	2433	0.43	25
3961	1.98	17	2491	0.07	34
3982	2.65	87	2499	1.11	14
3987	2.54	22	2611	0.13	48
3995	2.62	31	2621	0.52	26
\multicolumn{3}{l}{Sample size = 36}	2631	0.51	27

Appendix B (continued)

Standard Industrial Classification	Advertising-to-Sales Ratio (in percents)	Concentration Ratio (in percents)	Standard Industrial Classification	Advertising-to-Sales Ratio (in percents)	Concentration Ratio (in percents)
3576	0.31	54	2033	3.59	24
3579	0.13	35	2035	11.26	36
3582	0.28	59	2036	1.02	25
3583	0.00	77	2037	2.51	24
3586	0.26	49	2043	22.02	86
3589	0.04	34	2044	1.50	44
3611	0.27	22	2045	5.85	70
3613	0.33	61	2051	1.26	23
3615	0.27	73	2052	2.07	59
3617	0.26	46	2071	5.88	15
3619	0.27	34	2072	1.14	75
3664	0.27	96	2073	3.81	90
3669	0.33	55	2082	8.10	34
3693	0.51	58	2084	3.95	44
3715	0.58	56	2085	6.95	58
3721	0.61	53	2086	5.02	12
3722	0.28	72	2095	4.72	52
3723	0.38	98	2096	4.40	42
3729	0.38	37	2098	3.53	31
3731	0.00	43	2099	5.61	24
3741	0.19	91	2111	5.73	80
3742	0.01	56	2121	5.24	59
3799	0.21	37	2131	1.43	58
3841	0.31	39	2251	1.08	34
3843	8.51	40	2252	1.02	18
3997	0.25	54	2253	0.56	11
			2254	0.42	33
			2259	0.06	34
			2647	0.92	62
			2771	0.45	57
			2841	8.60	72
			2842	17.57	34
			2844	29.96	38
2011	0.22	31	3021	1.26	62
2013	0.61	16	3141	0.98	25
2015	0.32	14	3142	0.98	20
2021	0.39	11	3151	1.65	22
2022	0.87	44	3171	1.47	11
2023	2.19	40	3172	2.29	31
2024	1.35	37	3199	3.58	17
2026	0.55	23	3941	6.14	15
2031	2.42	38	3983	2.45	71
2032	5.62	67			

Sample size = 52

1963

Consumer Nondurables

Appendix B (continued)

Standard Industrial Classification	Advertising-to-Sales Ratio (in percents)	Concentration Ratio (in percents)	Standard Industrial Classification	Advertising-to-Sales Ratio (in percents)	Concentration Ratio (in percents)
3351	0.06	60	3872	0.27	40
3352	0.18	94	3912	0.19	39
3359	0.17	58	3933	4.07	71
3361	0.05	26	3952	0.27	51
3391	0.26	24	3953	0.36	16
3399	0.20	28	3954	0.23	56
3411	0.17	78	3955	0.25	32
3422	0.06	27	3962	0.30	10
3423	0.31	20	3963	5.76	20
3424	0.37	92	3964	0.32	34
3425	0.30	66	3981	0.49	22
3431	0.05	35	3982	0.20	82
3441	0.74	23	3993	0.31	5
3443	0.25	18			
3444	0.00	21	Sample size = 134		
3463	0.75	17			
3465	0.34	23	*Producer Durables*		
3466	0.27	33	2521	9.78	21
3467	0.38	38	2522	11.09	50
3468	0.33	15	2541	8.91	20
3471	0.33	18	2591	0.27	23
3489	0.12	20	3229	0.67	51
3491	0.18	52	3492	0.31	82
3493	0.24	43	3511	0.29	88
3494	0.30	20	3521	0.05	67
3495	0.31	17	3522	0.62	36
3496	0.30	53	3531	0.24	18
3499	0.26	31	3532	0.29	33
3561	0.76	29	3541	1.09	20
3564	0.50	39	3542	0.00	23
3585	3.58	39	3551	0.28	18
3591	0.30	24	3552	0.01	30
3592	0.24	22	3554	0.26	28
3593	0.03	62	3555	0.32	31
3612	0.28	87	3562	0.32	63
3614	0.28	59	3563	0.28	29
3631	0.16	41	3565	0.24	57
3641	0.75	67	3566	0.32	25
3651	1.30	92	3567	0.25	31
3662	0.36	73	3568	0.78	55
3691	0.47	62	3569	0.88	14
3842	5.27	58	3571	0.02	69
3861	2.09	61	3572	0.08	79

Appendix B (continued)

Standard Industrial Classification	Advertising-to-Sales Ratio (in percents)	Concentration Ratio (in percents)	Standard Industrial Classification	Advertising-to-Sales Ratio (in percents)	Concentration Ratio (in percents)
3986	0.30	35	2826	0.26	80
3987	0.25	21	2851	0.98	27
3992	0.40	33	2861	0.22	73
3996	0.27	52	2862	0.30	86
			2865	0.17	61
Sample size = 34			2881	0.10	43
			2882	0.10	75
Producer Nondurables			2883	0.09	44
2041	1.75	29	2884	0.11	41
2042	0.20	19	2886	0.19	29
2061	0.95	36	2887	0.12	68
2062	0.06	70	2891	0.22	57
2063	0.22	68	2892	0.17	63
2083	0.10	49	2895	0.29	78
2091	0.76	83	2896	0.34	83
2094	0.31	77	2898	1.73	81
2095	0.24	50	2911	0.63	37
2097	0.40	22	2932	0.01	53
2141	0.46	88	2951	0.22	19
2291	0.20	56	2952	0.19	42
2292	0.32	26	3031	0.29	84
2293	0.19	41	3099	0.02	30
2294	0.19	23	3111	0.18	27
2295	0.15	34	3121	0.23	44
2393	0.09	53	3131	0.14	30
2394	0.22	10	3221	0.17	63
2399	0.01	15	3241	0.01	30
2421	0.40	5	3271	0.13	8
2422	0.27	20	3272	0.26	85
2424	0.24	59	3274	0.26	30
2425	0.27	67	3275	0.25	57
2431	0.02	7	3281	0.33	8
2432	0.26	22	3291	0.27	49
2433	0.72	16	3292	0.26	58
2445	0.14	47	3293	0.26	42
2491	0.14	31	3297	0.03	62
2492	0.30	51	3311	0.09	67
2493	0.31	26	3312	0.23	45
2499	0.01	9	3321	0.35	16
2611	0.21	28	3323	0.32	23
2812	0.27	70	3333	0.19	53
2823	0.20	44	3334	0.10	100
2825	0.31	78	3341	0.08	41

Appendix B

FOUR-DIGIT SIC INDUSTRIES CLASSIFIED INTO SUBSAMPLES, 1947, 1963, AND 1967

Standard Industrial Classification	Advertising-to-Sales Ratio (in percents)	Concentration Ratio (in percents)	Standard Industrial Classification	Advertising-to-Sales Ratio (in percents)	Concentration Ratio (in percents)
	1947				
Consumer Nondurables			3984	0.22	51
2015	0.12	32	3985	0.26	43
2031	1.65	29	3994	1.06	27
2032	0.32	39	3995	0.20	22
2033	2.65	27			
2034	0.97	56	Sample size = 41		
2035	4.22	33			
2043	7.77	79	*Consumer Durables*		
2044	0.28	33	2271	2.55	52
2045	5.53	41	2273	1.27	25
2051	0.55	16	2274	1.16	80
2052	0.47	72	2391	0.46	18
2071	2.68	17	2392	0.65	33
2072	1.68	68	2514	0.76	26
2073	0.55	70	2515	0.11	36
2081	3.01	10	2563	0.12	15
2082	2.84	21	3161	2.27	15
2084	5.82	26	3421	2.36	41
2085	9.15	75	3581	2.19	40
2092	1.02	59	3584	2.57	61
2093	1.88	64	3621	2.10	36
2098	0.63	23	3661	3.07	26
2111	6.00	90	3663	0.71	79
2121	5.54	41	3716	1.04	17
2131	5.61	61	3717	2.07	56
2893	34.35	24	3732	2.30	31
3011	1.11	77	3751	0.08	42
3021	1.42	81	3851	0.32	58
3141	1.14	28	3871	2.75	41
3171	0.01	7	3911	2.85	13
3172	0.13	28	3913	0.54	26
3192	0.44	33	3914	5.80	61
3199	2.46	15	3931	2.76	46
3692	0.09	76	3932	6.53	78
3941	1.00	20	3939	2.89	24
3942	0.26	39	3943	0.23	30
3949	4.75	24	3951	1.69	58
3983	0.26	83	3961	2.62	24

74

i Douglas F. Greer, "Advertising and Market Concentration," *Southern Economic Journal*, vol. 38 (July 1971), pp. 19-32.

k H. M. Mann, J. A. Henning, and J. W. Meehan, Jr., "Advertising and Market Concentration: Comment," *Southern Economic Journal*, vol. 39 (January 1973), pp. 448–451.

l Franklin R. Edwards, "Advertising and Competition in Banking," *Antitrust Bulletin*, vol. 18 (Spring 1973), pp. 23–32.

m John Cable, "Market Structure, Advertising Policy, and Intermarket Differences in Advertising Intensity," *Market Structure and Corporate Behavior*, Keith Cowling, ed. (London: Gray-Mills Ltd., 1972), pp. 105–124.

n Stanley I. Ornstein, J. Fred Weston, Michael Intriligator, and Ronald Shrieves, "Determinants of Market Structure," *Southern Economic Journal*, vol. 39 (April 1973), pp. 612–625.

o C. J. Sutton, "Advertising, Concentration, and Competition," *Economic Journal*, vol. 84 (March 1974), pp. 56–69.

p Willard F. Mueller and Larry G. Hamm, "Trends in Industrial Market Concentration, 1947 to 1970," *Review of Economics and Statistics*, vol. 56 (November 1974), pp. 511–520.

q W. Duncan Reekie, "Advertising and Market Structure: Another Approach," *Economic Journal*, vol. 85 (March 1975), pp. 156–164.

r R. D. Rees, "Advertising, Concentration, and Competition: A Comment and Further Results," *Economic Journal*, vol. 85 (March 1975), pp. 165–174.

s Phillip Nelson, "The Economic Consequences of Advertising," *Journal of Business*, vol. 48 (April 1975), pp. 213–241.

t Jean-Jacques Lambin, *Advertising, Competition, and Market Conduct in Oligopoly over Time: An Econometric Investigation in Western European Countries* (Amsterdam: North-Holland, 1976).

u Brian C. Brush, "The Influence of Market Structure on Industry Advertising Intensity," *Journal of Industrial Economics*, vol. 25 (September 1976), pp. 55–67.

v David J. Theroux, "Marcus' 'Advertising and Changes in Concentration': A Comment," unpublished paper, University of Chicago, 1976.

w Allyn D. Strickland and Leonard W. Weiss, "Advertising, Concentration, and Price-Cost Margins," *Journal of Political Economy*, vol. 84 (October 1976), pp. 1109–1121.

Appendix A (continued)

Study	Sample	Period	Dependent Variable	Independent Variable	Functional Form	Statistical Significance
Strickland and Weiss (1976)[w]	408 SIC four-digit industries	1963	Advertising-sales ratio	Four-firm concentration	Quadratic	Significant
			Four-firm concentration	Advertising-sales ratio	Linear	Significant

Note: Certain studies had other independent variables such as market growth and various proxies for barriers to entry.

[a] Lester G. Telser, "Advertising and Competition," *Journal of Political Economy*, vol. 72 (December 1964), pp. 537–562.

[b] H. M. Mann, J. A. Henning, and J. W. Meehan, Jr., "Advertising and Concentration: An Empirical Investigation," *Journal of Industrial Economics*, vol. 16 (November 1967), pp. 34–45.

[c] Peter Doyle, "Advertising Expenditure and Consumer Demand," *Oxford Economic Papers*, vol. 20 (November 1968), pp. 394–416.

[d] Lester G. Telser, "Another Look at Advertising and Concentration," *Journal of Industrial Economics*, vol. 18 (November 1969), pp. 85–94.

[e] Robert B. Ekelund, Jr., and Charles Maurice, "An Empirical Investigation of Advertising and Concentration: Comment," *Journal of Industrial Economics*, vol. 18 (November 1969), pp. 76–80.

[f] Matityahu Marcus, "Advertising and Changes in Concentration," *Southern Economic Journal*, vol. 36 (October 1969), pp. 117–121.

[g] Robert B. Ekelund, Jr., and William P. Gramm, "Advertising and Concentration: Some New Evidence," *Antitrust Bulletin*, vol. 5 (Summer 1970), pp. 243–249.

[h] Louis Guth, "Advertising and Market Structure Revisited," *Journal of Industrial Economics*, vol. 19 (April 1971), pp. 179–198.

[i] John M. Vernon, "Concentration, Promotion, and Market Share Stability in the Pharmaceutical Industry," *Journal of Industrial Economics*, vol. 19 (July 1971), pp. 246–266.

Study	Sample	Period	Dependent/Independent variable	Concentration measure	Functional form	Results
Rees (1975)[r]	Sutton's sample (Great Britain)	1963, 1968	Advertising-sales ratio (including and excluding excise taxes)	Five-firm concentration ratio	Linear and quadratic	Significant when taxes are included
Nelson (1975)[s]	41 IRS consumer goods divided into experience durable, nondurable and search goods	1958	Advertising-sales ratio	Four-firm concentration ratio	Linear	Insignificant for experience durable and nondurable goods, significant for search goods
Lambin (1976)[t]	Six subsamples drawn from 107 brands of consumer goods in Western European countries	1960–1970	Herfindahl index, three-firm and five-firm concentration ratios	Advertising-sales ratio and advertising per inhabitant	Linear	Insignificantly positive in five out of six samples
Brush (1976)[u]	28 SIC four-digit industries	1954–1963	Weighted average dominant firm advertising-sales ratio	Four-firm concentration	Linear Quadratic	Significant Insignificant
Theroux (1976)[v]	78 and 61 SIC four-digit consumer goods industries	1947–1963	Change in four- and eight-firm concentration	Dummy variables for high and medium product differentiation based on advertising intensity	Linear	Significant in certain periods for 78 industry sample; insignificant for 61 industry sample

Appendix A (continued)

Study	Sample	Period	Dependent Variable	Independent Variable	Functional Form	Statistical Significance
Cable (1972)[m]	26 narrowly defined consumer goods industries (Great Britain)	1963	Advertising-sales ratio and stock of advertising-to-sales ratio	Three-firm concentration ratio and Herfindahl index	Linear and quadratic	Mixed depending on functional form
Ornstein, Weston, Intriligator, and Shrieves (1973)[n]	113 IRS industries	1963	Four-firm concentration	Advertising Advertising-sales ratio	Log	Significant Significant
Sutton (1974)[o]	25 consumer goods industries (Great Britain)	1963	Advertising-sales ratio (inclusive of excise taxes)	Five-firm concentration	Linear Quadratic	Insignificant Significant
Mueller and Hamm (1974)[p]	166 SIC four-digit industries	1947–1970	Change in four-firm concentration	High, moderate, and low advertising intensive dummy variables	Linear	Significant for high and moderate
Reekie (1975)[q]	63 nondurable consumer goods industries (Great Britain)	1971	Advertising-sales ratio	Three-firm and five-firm density ratios	Linear Quadratic	Insignificant Insignificant

Study	Sample	Years	Concentration measure	Functional form	Results
Ekelund and Gramm (1970)[g]	39 IRS three-digit consumer goods industries	1963	Four-firm concentration	Linear	Insignificant; change in concentration also insignificant
Guth (1971)[h]	35 IRS three-digit consumer goods industries	1958, 1963	Four-firm concentration / Lorenz coefficient	Linear and log / Linear	Insignificant except for linear regression using Lorenz coefficient
Vernon (1971)[i]	18 therapeutic product classes	1964, 1968	Four-firm concentration / Herfindahl index	Linear / Linear	Insignificant / Insignificant
Greer (1971)[j]	41 IRS three-digit consumer goods industries, divided into three classes of product differentiability	1947, 1954, and 1958	Advertising-sales ratio	Quadratic	Significant and insignificant, depending on sample tested
Mann, Henning, and Meehan (1973)[k]	Greer's samples less one industry in each class	1947, 1954, and 1958	Advertising-sales ratio	Quadratic	Generally insignificant
Edwards (1973)[l]	36 national banks	1964, 1965	Three-firm concentration ratio / Advertising-sales ratio	Linear	Insignificant

Appendix A
A SURVEY OF CONCENTRATION-ADVERTISING INTENSITY STUDIES

Study	Sample	Period	Dependent Variable	Independent Variable	Functional Form	Statistical Significance
Telser (1964)[a]	42 IRS three-digit consumer goods industries	1947, 1954, and 1958	Four-firm concentration	Advertising-sales ratio	Linear	Insignificant in each year; first differences also insignificant
Mann, Henning, and Meehan (1967)[b]	14 SIC four-digit industries	1954, 1958, and 1963	Four-firm concentration	Average dominant firm advertising-sales ratio	Linear	Significant in each year
Doyle (1968)[c]	85 trades (Great Britain)	1958	Advertising-sales ratio	Three-firm advertising concentration	Linear	Insignificant
Telser (1969)[d]	26 four-digit SIC industries	1958	Four-firm concentration	Average dominant firm advertising-sales ratio	Linear	Insignificant
Ekelund and Maurice (1969)[e]	Mann et al. sample	1954–1963	Change in four-firm concentration	Change in advertising-sales ratio	Linear	Insignificant
Marcus (1969)[f]	78 SIC four-digit consumer goods industries	1947–1963	Change in four-firm concentration	High, medium, or low advertising intensity dummy variable	Linear	Significant for high and medium coefficients

APPENDIX

Appendix A: A Survey of Concentration-Advertising Intensity Studies

Appendix B: Four-Digit SIC Industries Classified into Subsamples, 1947, 1963, and 1967

Similarly, in the ready-to-eat (RTE) cereals case, the FTC charges respondents with artificially differentiating

> their RTE cereals. Respondents produce basically similar RTE cereals, and then emphasize and exaggerate trivial variations such as color and shape. Respondents employ trademarks to conceal such basic similarities and to differentiate cereal brands. Respondents also use premiums to induce purchases of RTE cereals.
>
> These practices of proliferating brands, differentiating similar products and promoting trademarks through intensive advertising result in high barriers to entry into the RTE cereal market.[4]

These positions reflect clearly the contradictions inherent in arguing that advertising is an agent of both competition and monopoly. In one case, sellers (pharmacists) have allegedly curbed competition by suppressing advertising, while in the other cases, sellers (a maker of reconstituted lemon juice and the largest four makers of ready-to-eat cereals) have allegedly used advertising itself to restrict competition. How advertising can be part of the competitive process for some goods but not for others—or how such a distinction can be made in practice—is yet to be explained. Until it is explained, the FTC may be characterized as exhibiting a puzzling ambivalence toward advertising. The commission can recognize, as it has in the investigation of advertising by pharmacists, that competition, including advertising competition, promotes consumer welfare. Or it can revert, as it threatens to do in the ReaLemon and cereals cases, to its long tradition of protecting competitors at the expense of competition and of consumer welfare.

---

[4] Kellogg Company, General Mills, Inc., General Foods Corporation, and the Quaker Oats Company Complaint, Docket No. 8883, Federal Trade Commission, April 1972, pp. 5, 6.

theory and the evidence before we can conclude that advertising adversely affects competition and misallocates resources.

The introduction noted that a series of recent antitrust actions has challenged the long-established ban on advertising for professional services such as pharmacy, optometry, law, and medicine. In the FTC staff investigation of prescription drugs, it was claimed that the moving force behind restraints on price advertising

> appears to be conscious parallel behavior and concerted efforts by the major organizations purporting to represent pharmacists on the national level. . . . Information . . . suggests that the motivation underlying such cooperative behavior is not rooted primarily in a concern for the public health and welfare, but . . . stems from a common interest in insulating the practice of pharmacy from the normal economic pressures and perils of the marketplace.[2]

In other words, advertising would be competitive and in the public interest.

Here, by contrast, is the FTC's initial decision on the effects of advertising in the ReaLemon case:

> The high, in fact, extreme, degree of brand dominance attained by ReaLemon over the years [through advertising] indicates, in itself, a power over prices and entry. Dr. Michael Mann made a study of product differentiation as a barrier to entry.
>
> In Dr. Mann's opinion where high product differentiation is present ". . . one should expect to find high market concentration; one should expect to find levels of profitability which are persistently, noticeably and markedly above those earned by firms in the general class of economic activities in which they operate, and that this dominance is not easily subject to erosion."
>
> Respondent's ReaLemon is differentiated from other brands to such a degree as to be virtually the generic name for the product itself. Such differentiation, the attendant dominant market share, coupled with the high profitability and premium price commanded by ReaLemon have given, and now give, respondent Borden a substantial measure of power over industry prices and the ability to restrict competition and competitive entry.[3]

---

[2] Quoted in John F. Cady, *Restricted Advertising and Competition: The Case of Retail Drugs* (Washington, D.C.: American Enterprise Institute, 1976), p. 3.

[3] Borden, Inc., Case, Docket No. 8978, Federal Trade Commission, August 19, 1976, pp. 75-77.

The sample tested in this study was selected in order to mitigate the problems that were the subject of criticism in previous efforts. The results indicate that there is a significant (but weak) positive, linear relationship, with no apparent quadratic relationship, and that (unexpectedly) concentration and advertising intensity are weakly related in producer as well as consumer goods markets. This latter finding undermines the barrier-to-entry argument and suggests that the positive relationship is explained in large part by spurious correlation. Finally, the insignificant quadratic relationship provides no support for the belief that excess advertising expenditures occur in oligopolistic industries or for the belief that there is a lack of advertising competition as a result of collusion.

A number of unresolved econometric problems make results based on a simple univariate relationship further suspect. For example, there is a specification problem in all studies inasmuch as a number of variables that are not taken into account may be expected to influence both advertising intensity and concentration. Factors such as the rate of new product introduction, consumer search costs, size of market, and product characteristics such as durability, technological complexity, and price are strong determinants of the level of advertising. Factors such as market size, capital intensity, and economies of scale are strong determinants of the level of concentration. With few exceptions, little attempt has been made to account for other determinants of advertising intensity and concentration. If one or more of these unaccounted-for variables is independently related to advertising intensity and concentration, it may be impossible to tell how an observed positive correlation between advertising intensity and concentration arises. Finally, the potential simultaneous effects exerted by advertising intensity and concentration on each other lead to a positive relationship. Obviously, a simple two-variable model is naive, and any results from such a model should be interpreted with extreme care. A host of alternative explanations may account for any relationship that appears to exist, and there is no way at present to distinguish between them.

Certainly there is no basis for concluding that advertising leads to a decrease in competition. The simple relationship (or lack of relationship) between concentration and advertising intensity now available provides no theoretical or empirical support for recommending any public policy. There is no basis whatever for concluding, as some have, that heavily advertised products should be closely scrutinized for evidence of antitrust violations merely because they are heavily advertised. We need far greater understanding of both the

4
CONCLUSION

Let us briefly summarize our findings. First, we have seen that the traditional (Kaldor-Bain) view that advertising causes industrial concentration has little empirical support. Second, we have seen that the new learning (that causality runs the other way or possibly both ways) has mixed empirical support. And third, we have examined a new set of empirical tests that reduce the scope for error, but that nevertheless yield ambiguous results—none of those results being strong enough to support the argument that advertising reduces competition.

There is little evidence for economies of scale in advertising, or for the view that advertising creates brand loyalty, two of the key foundations for the barriers-to-entry hypothesis. As we have seen, the results of regressions involving concentration and advertising intensity are at best inconclusive. All previous studies, whether they find a significant positive relationship or none at all, are subject to strong criticism for measurement error and poor statistical technique. Studies using IRS data, which tend to reject a simple linear relationship, show a significant but weak positive relationship when rank correlation is used or when the variables are transformed into logarithms. The finding of a strong positive relationship by Mann, Henning, and Meehan was shown by Telser to be a result of the sample selected: a more comprehensive sample of firms and industries showed no significant relationship. In like manner, the findings of a significant quadratic relationship were subsequently shown to be the result of sample selection and measurement error, the correction of which resulted in no support for a quadratic relationship.[1]

---

[1] The one exception is the Strickland and Weiss study, which is too new to have generated critical responses. It remains a puzzle how they found a significant quadratic relationship using input-output data for 1963 and this author did not. Part of the difference in results may lie in the different samples used and the different ways advertising intensity was measured.

Summary

Most advocates of the position that advertising leads to monopoly power concede that it could do so only in consumer goods industries with large advertising expenditures. They also recognize that advertising is related to such other factors as product characteristics, buyer search costs, frequency of purchase, and behavior of rival firms, so that advertising can be a potential barrier to entry only in a certain subset of consumer goods industries usually left unspecified. The usual test of this hypothesis is to correlate industry advertising intensity with either concentration ratios or profit rates as proxies for monopoly power for all consumer goods industries. A positive correlation generally leads to the assertion that advertising creates product differentiation and is a barrier to entry.

Compared with most previous studies, the sample used here is larger and therefore less subject to sampling bias. It uses disaggregated four-digit industries that more closely approximate economic markets and that are less subject to aggregation bias, and it uses a well-defined basis for identifying consumer and producer goods industries. Contrary to several of these studies, we found that (1) concentration and advertising are weakly correlated in both consumer *and* producer goods industries and (2) there is no evidence of a quadratic relationship between concentration and advertising. The fact that the results are similar for consumer and producer nondurable goods industries suggests the existence of spurious correlation from large-firm effects. Although this finding does not disprove the existence of advertising barriers to entry in consumer nondurables it makes that existence suspect. There is no basis for a positive correlation in producer goods industries according to the traditional theory; yet one exists. By inference, the finding of a positive correlation in consumer goods is just as likely not due to advertising as a barrier to entry.

Table 9
MEAN ADVERTISING INTENSITY BY CONCENTRATION DECILES, 1967

Sample	Concentration Decile										Mean	N
	0-9	10-19	20-29	30-39	40-49	50-59	60-69	70-79	80-89	90-100		
Total	0.6	0.8	1.2	2.1	1.7	2.7	1.6	2.6	3.6	1.0c	1.7	324
Consumer	1.0a	1.7	2.1	5.5	3.3	4.8	4.7	5.3	6.7	d	3.8	87
Producer	0.5	0.5	0.8	1.1	1.0	0.9	0.9	1.3	1.9	1.0	0.9	237
Consumer nondurable	1.0a	2.0	2.3	6.2	3.8	4.9	2.8	7.3b	7.5	d	4.1	54
Consumer durable	d	1.1	1.6	3.9	2.8	4.6	8.5b	3.9c	3.7a	d	3.3	33
Producer nondurable	0.6	0.6	0.8	1.1	1.0	1.0	1.0	1.3	1.0	2.5a	0.9	184
Producer durable	0.4a	0.4	0.9	0.9	0.8	0.6	0.6	d	3.7c	0.3b	0.9	53

a One industry.
b Two industries.
c Three industries.
d No industries fell in this category.

Table 8
MEAN ADVERTISING INTENSITY BY CONCENTRATION DECILES, 1963

Sample	Concentration Decile										Mean	N
	0-9	10-19	20-29	30-39	40-49	50-59	60-69	70-79	80-89	90-100		
Total	0.6	1.0	1.2	2.3	1.6	1.5	2.1	2.1	4.2	1.3	1.7	329
Consumer	d	2.1	2.0	5.6	3.4	3.3	5.8	3.8	8.4	3.8[a]	3.8	90
Producer	0.6	0.5	0.9	0.9	1.1	0.8	0.9	1.0	0.8	0.9	0.9	239
Consumer nondurable	d	2.5	2.1	6.2	2.6	3.5	2.6[c]	4.5	13.9[b]	3.8[a]	4.0	54
Consumer durable	d	1.2	1.9	4.5	4.3	3.1	10.5[b]	2.8[c]	3.0[b]	d	3.4	36
Producer nondurable	0.6	0.5	1.0	0.8	1.0	0.9	1.1	1.0	0.8	1.5[c]	0.9	189
Producer durable	0.4[a]	0.3	0.8	1.4	1.2	0.6	0.5[c]	1.1[a]	d	0.3[c]	0.8	50

[a] One industry.
[b] Two industries.
[c] Three industries.
[d] No industries fell in this category.

Table 7
MEAN ADVERTISING INTENSITY BY CONCENTRATION DECILES, 1947

Sample	Concentration Decile										Mean	N
	0-9	10-19	20-29	30-39	40-49	50-59	60-69	70-79	80-89	90-100		
Total	0.2	0.8	1.9	0.6	1.2	0.9	1.0	1.5	0.6	1.1	1.1	261
Consumer	0.02[a]	1.7	3.6	0.9	2.7	1.1	3.5	3.3	0.9[c]	6.0[a]	2.4	75
Producer	0.2	0.4	1.0	0.4	0.6	0.8	0.3	0.5	0.5	0.4	0.6	186
Consumer nondurable	0.02[a]	2.2	4.7	0.9	3.8[c]	0.7[c]	3.1[c]	3.2	0.8[b]	6.0[a]	2.9	41
Consumer durable	[d]	1.3	1.6	0.9	2.0	1.4	4.2[b]	3.6[b]	1.2[a]	[d]	1.7	34
Producer nondurable	0.2	0.3	0.6	0.5	0.2	0.5	0.4	0.6	0.5	0.5	0.4	134
Producer durable	[d]	0.5[c]	2.4	0.3	2.3	1.3	0.2	0.2	0.3[b]	0.3[c]	1.0	52

[a] One industry.
[b] Two industries.
[c] Three industries.
[d] No industries fell in this category.

brand loyalty, they make the traditional interpretation highly suspect.

The quadratic relationship receives no empirical support in any of the regression equations. The concentration-squared term is generally negative, consistent with an inverse relationship at high levels of concentration, but it is significant only for all producer goods industries—which, again, is not in accordance with conventional expectations. The negative coefficient and the lack of significance may be the result of interdependence among the supposedly independent variables (multicollinearity), if the range in which the concentration ratio (CR) and the concentration ratio squared (CR^2) are measured is approximately linear. Collinearity is quite high (over 90 percent) in most subsamples, and rounding error may lead to the negative term. When the squared term alone is regressed on advertising, it turns out to be significant and positively related.[18]

Two tests for a quadratic relationship were made. The results of the first test, which attempted to circumvent part of the collinearity problem, did not show an inverse relationship at high levels of concentration.[19] In the second test, average advertising-to-sales ratios were calculated by concentration deciles to see if a quadratic pattern could be observed. The results seen in Tables 7, 8, and 9 are difficult to evaluate because certain categories have been strongly affected by one or two industries. However, in the consumer goods subsamples there is no discernible negative relationship at higher concentration levels in any year. If anything, there appears to be a U, or a bimodal, rather than an inverted-U relationship in certain years. Hence, we can safely conclude that we have found no strong empirical support in these results for the view that moderately concentrated industries overinvest in advertising relative to other industries or that highly concentrated industries collude to reduce advertising intensity.

---

[18] This study focused on the quadratic relationship because it has received the most attention in the literature. Other nonlinear models estimated were:

$$ASR = a_5 + b_5 CR^2 + e_5$$
$$\text{Log } ASR = a_6 + b_6 \text{Log} CR + e_6$$

Essentially, the same pattern of results obtained, although the log-log model generally gave a higher R^2 in consumer goods subsamples than the linear model.

[19] Slope dummy variables were used in both linear and logarithmic form, dividing the samples at the 60 percent concentration level. The 60 percent level was chosen as the intermediate concentration level where advertising intensity should be maximum, based on the quadratic results and theoretical arguments in previous studies. In effect, this technique estimates two separate regressions; one over the concentration range of 0 to 60 and another from 60 to 100 percent. By forcing the regression into two components, the collinearity observed with a single continuous function may be reduced.

					R^2
Producer Nondurable N = 184	−5.0470	.0069* (1.97)		.9410** (15.20)	.56
	−5.1522	.0125 (0.90)	−.0001 (0.42)	.9430** (15.10)	.56
Producer Durable N = 53	−2.7715	.0030 (0.53)		.6064** (5.05)	.33
	−2.9171	.0095 (0.42)	−.0001 (0.30)	.6097** (5.01)	.32

R^2 (coefficient of determination)—Adjusted for degrees of freedom.
t—Ratio in parentheses.
*—Significant at .05 level.
**—Significant at .01 level.

Table 6
REGRESSIONS OF ADVERTISING EXPENDITURES (LOG) ON CONCENTRATION AND SALES (LOG) BY PRODUCT CATEGORIES, 1967

Sample	Intercept	Coefficient of Concentration	Coefficient of Squared Concentration	LOG Sales	Coefficient of Determination
Total N = 324	−4.7894	.0119** (3.86)		.9264** (16.52)	.46
	−5.0773	.0260* (2.10)	−.0002 (1.18)	.9332** (16.55)	.46
Consumer N = 87	−4.3846	.0212** (4.22)		.9609** (10.63)	.58
	−5.0722	.0516** (2.33)	−.0003 (1.41)	.9802** (10.77)	.58
Producer N = 237	−4.5948	.0054* (1.80)		.8763** (15.94)	.52
	−4.7394	.0127 (1.08)	−.0001 (0.64)	.8796** (15.91)	.52
Consumer Nondurable N = 54	−4.3280	.0199** (2.70)		.9597** (7.41)	.52
	−4.9114	.0486 (1.49)	−.0003 (0.90)	.9690** (7.45)	.52
Consumer Durable N = 33	−4.5534	.0235** (4.20)		.9722** (8.41)	.70
	−5.5201	.0590 (2.42)	−.0004 (1.49)	1.0196** (8.66)	.72

					R^2
Producer Nondurable $N = 189$	−7.1854	.0068* (2.03)		1.1324** (17.49)	.62
	−7.4463	.0174 (1.38)	−.0001 (0.87)	1.1388** (17.47)	.62
Producer Durable $N = 50$	−2.0936	−.0012 (0.43)		.7595** (5.91)	.40
	−2.5400	.0255 (1.10)	−.0003 (1.19)	.7541** (5.89)	.41

R^2 (coefficient of determination)—Adjusted for degrees of freedom.
t—Ratio in parentheses.
*—Significant at .05 level.
**—Significant at .01 level.

Table 5
REGRESSIONS OF ADVERTISING EXPENDITURES (LOG) ON CONCENTRATION AND SALES (LOG) BY PRODUCT CATEGORIES, 1963

Sample	Intercept	Coefficient of Concentration	Coefficient of Squared Concentration	LOG Sales	Coefficient of Determination
Total N = 329	−6.0908	.0091** (2.95)		1.0680** (18.81)	.52
	−6.4732	.0247* (2.05)	−.0002 (1.34)	1.0765** (18.87)	.52
Consumer N = 90	−4.9526	.0181** (3.31)		1.0301** (11.67)	.61
	−5.2753	.0306 (1.22)	−.0001 (0.51)	1.0377** (11.55)	.61
Producer N = 239	−6.0146	.0041 (1.37)		1.0481** (18.09)	.58
	−6.3518	.0182* (1.65)	−.0002 (1.33)	1.0554** (18.16)	.58
Consumer Nondurable N = 54	−6.5661	.0203** (2.66)		1.1455 (8.74)	.59
	−6.4464	.0142 (0.42)	.0001 (0.18)	1.1446 (8.64)	.58
Consumer Durable N = 36	−7.1854	.0068* (2.03)		1.1324** (17.49)	.62
	−7.4463	.0174 (1.38)	−.0001 (0.87)	1.1388** (17.47)	.62

					R^2
Producer Nondurable $N = 134$	−4.8704 −4.7315	.0038 (0.88) −.0037 (0.20)		.0001 (0.42)	.8844** (11.22) .8843** (11.18)	.49 .49
Producer Durable $N = 52$	1.7968 3.2310	−.0153 (1.41) −.0617 (1.22)		.0004 (0.94)	.4106* (1.73) .3763 (1.56)	.09 .08

R^2 (coefficient of determination)—Adjusted for degrees of freedom.
t—Ratio in parentheses.
*—Significant at .05 level.
**—Significant at .01 level.

Table 4
REGRESSIONS OF ADVERTISING EXPENDITURES (LOG) ON CONCENTRATION AND SALES (LOG) BY PRODUCT CATEGORIES, 1947

Sample	Intercept	Coefficient of Concentration	Coefficient of Squared Concentration	LOG Sales	Coefficient of Determination
Total $N = 261$	−4.9380	−.0000 (0.00)		.9418** (12.33)	.37
	−4.9024	−.0016 (0.09)	.0000 (0.09)	.9414** (12.25)	.37
Consumer $N = 75$	−8.7636	.0074 (1.04)		1.3257** (11.45)	.65
	−9.0252	.0179 (0.51)	−.0001 (0.30)	1.3314** (11.27)	.64
Producer $N = 186$	−3.4652	−.0011 (0.26)		.7880** (9.61)	.34
	−3.2907	−.0091 (0.49)	.0001 (0.45)	.7863** (9.56)	.34
Consumer Nondurable $N = 41$	−9.4692	.0045 (0.45)		1.3909** (8.74)	.66
	−10.9744	.0527 (0.99)	−.0005 (0.92)	1.4427** (8.56)	.66
Consumer Durable $N = 34$	−7.6189	.0133 (1.24)		1.2134** (6.79)	.59
	−7.2908	−.0259 (0.50)	.0004 (0.77)	1.2469** (6.74)	.59

interval, in comparison to the current mean ratio in all industries of 1.7 percent. For all consumer goods a doubling of concentration would yield a ratio within the range of 1.8 to 5.7 percent at the 95 percent confidence interval, compared with the existing mean ratio of 3.8 percent.

The linear results are consistent with both of the nontraditional hypotheses suggested above, pp. 39–42. The first of these hypotheses (whereby advertising is a means of entry) predicts a stronger relationship between advertising and concentration for consumer goods than for producer goods and a stronger relationship between them for consumer nondurable goods than for consumer durable goods. The estimations for 1963 and 1967 yielded a stronger relationship for consumer goods than for producer goods, and the 1963 estimation yielded a stronger relationship for consumer nondurables than for consumer durables (though 1967 yielded opposite results). These estimations are consistent also with the traditional (Kaldor-Bain) hypothesis, the efficient firm hypothesis, and the argument that there will be more nonprice competition in highly concentrated industries. The existing data clearly do not reveal which of these various conflicting hypotheses is the most accurate.

The second nontraditional hypothesis suggested above holds that the positive relationship is a result of spurious correlation—that is, a "statistical artifact." This implies a positive relationship in both consumer and producer goods industries, while the traditional school of thought holds that the main causes of a positive relationship—economies of scale and capital barriers to entry as a result of advertising—would occur only in the highly advertising-intensive consumer goods industries. A positive relationship in producer goods industries must be explained on other grounds. The results for both 1963 and 1967 are consistent with the spurious correlation hypothesis. Concentration is significant in both consumer and producer nondurable goods industries. Advertising intensity is much smaller in producer nondurables than in consumer nondurables, with advertising averaging 0.9 percent of shipments versus 4.0 percent of shipments. Thus, the usual explanation of advertising economies of scale or advertising-created brand loyalty would seem to be highly unlikely. Moreover, producer nondurables have lower total advertising expenditures, yet concentration appears significant (in Tables 5 and 6) for both consumer and producer nondurable goods industries. These results do not *disprove* the traditional view as it applies to consumer goods industries, but, coupled with the general lack of evidence of significant advertising economies of scale or of advertising-created

Table 3
ADVERTISING INTENSITY AND CONCENTRATION REGRESSIONS, BY PRODUCT CATEGORY, 1967

Sample	Intercept	Coefficient of Concentration	Coefficient of Squared Concentration	Coefficient of Determination
Total	0.5946	.0282**		.05
N = 324		(3.92)		
	0.2651	.0472	−.0002	.04
		(1.63)	(0.68)	
Consumer	1.1313	.0646**		.10
N = 87		(3.05)		
	−0.1076	.1324	−.0007	.09
		(1.41)	(0.74)	
Producer	0.5788	.0089**		.02
N = 237		(2.44)		
	0.4793	.0147	−.0001	.02
		(1.04)	(0.43)	
Consumer	1.4926	.0644*		.08
Nondurable		(2.11)		
N = 54	0.4096	.1242	−.0006	.06
		(0.91)	(0.45)	
Consumer	0.3728	.0687**		.20
Durable		(2.81)		
N = 33	−1.5268	.1709	.0011	.20
		(1.56)	(0.96)	
Producer	0.6333	.0077*		.02
Nondurable		(1.95)		
N = 184	0.4474	.0191	−.0001	.02
		(1.21)	(0.75)	
Producer	0.3790	.0128		.04
Durable		(1.45)		
N = 53	0.4080	.0113	.0000	.02
		(0.32)	(0.14)	

R^2 (coefficient of determination)—Adjusted for degrees of freedom.
  t—Ratio in parentheses.
  *—Significant at .05 level.
  **—Significant at .01 level.

Table 2
ADVERTISING INTENSITY AND CONCENTRATION REGRESSIONS, BY PRODUCT CATEGORY, 1963

Sample	Intercept	Coefficient of Concentration	Coefficient of Squared Concentration	Coefficient of Determination
Total $N = 329$	0.9177	.0191** (2.45)		.02
	0.5086	.0428 (1.41)	−.0003 (0.80)	.01
Consumer $N = 90$	1.7509	.0509* (2.08)		.04
	0.9072	.0981 (0.89)	−.0005 (0.44)	.03
Producer $N = 239$	0.7050	.0040 (1.41)		.00
	0.4352	.0197* (1.89)	−.0002 (1.57)	.01
Consumer Nondurable $N = 54$	1.6641	.0606* (1.77)		.04
	2.3478	.0217 (0.14)	.0004 (0.26)	.02
Consumer Durable $N = 36$	1.8100	.0389 (1.14)		.01
	−1.5712	.2230 (1.43)	−.0020 (1.21)	.02
Producer Nondurable $N = 189$	0.6535	.0057* (1.89)		.01
	0.5234	.0136 (1.19)	−.0001 (0.72)	.01
Producer Durable $N = 50$	0.9054	−.0022 (0.30)		−.02
	0.2020	.0340 (1.26)	−.0004 (1.39)	.00

R^2 (coefficient of determination)—Adjusted for degrees of freedom.
t—Ratio in parentheses.
*—Significant at .05 level.
**—Significant at .01 level.

Table 1
ADVERTISING INTENSITY AND CONCENTRATION REGRESSIONS, BY PRODUCT CATEGORY, 1947

Sample	Intercept	Coefficient of Concentration	Coefficient of Squared Concentration	Coefficient of Determination
Total	1.3057	−.0045		.00
$N = 261$		(0.60)		
	1.3162	−.0050	.0000	.00
		(0.15)	(0.00)	
Consumer	2.1169	.0063		.00
$N = 75$		(0.27)		
	3.3376	−.0597	.0007	−.01
		(0.53)	(0.59)	
Producer				
$N = 186$	0.7854	−.0041		.00
		(0.86)		
	0.6291	.0040	−.0001	.00
		(0.19)	(0.40)	
Consumer	3.2444	−.0073		.00
Nondurable		(0.19)		
$N = 41$	4.4244	.0721	.0007	−.02
		(0.37)	(0.34)	
Consumer	0.7306	.0250*		.09
Durable		(1.82)		
$N = 34$	1.4532	−.0142	.0004	.08
		(0.22)	(0.06)	
Producer	0.3814	.0012		.00
Nondurable		(0.41)		
$N = 134$	0.3518	.0028	−.0000	−.01
		(0.22)	(0.13)	
Producer	2.1269	−.0232		.04
Durable		(1.47)		
$N = 52$	2.5669	−.0433	.0002	.02
		(0.59)	(0.28)	

R^2 (coefficient of determination)—Adjusted for degrees of freedom.
t—Ratio in parentheses.
*—Significant at .05 level.
**—Significant at .01 level.

The results for 1963 and 1967 are discussed together since they are similar to each other. Both Tables 2 and 3 show some significant positive linear relationships. There is no significant relationship in consumer and producer durable goods and in all producer goods for 1963. There is none in producer durable goods for 1967. A similar pattern—no linear relationship for 1947, but a positive linear relationship for 1963 and 1967—is supported by Tables 4, 5, and 6 with estimates of equation (3). The conclusion that there is a positive relationship must be qualified, however, since concentration explains practically none of the variation in advertising intensity. For 1963, in Table 2, the R^2 (coefficient of determination) is never more than 4 percent. A similarly low level of variation explained by concentration was evident for the log of total advertising expenditures in Table 5. Thus, even the significant relationships for 1963 are quite weak, with omitted variables explaining over 95 percent of the variation in advertising intensity and total advertising expenditures.

The linear results for 1967 are consistently more significant than those for 1963, with correspondingly higher R^2s. Nevertheless, with the exception of consumer durables, the unexplained variation is 90 percent or higher, indicating that omitted variables are far more important than concentration.[17]

These results are consistent with Telser's and Nelson's arguments that differences in advertising levels across industries are best explained by product characteristics, consumer demands for information, and the comparative cost of advertising messages and alternative forms of product promotion.

The size of coefficients in Table 2 suggests that the influence of concentration on advertising intensity is modest in most cases. For example, for the total 1963 sample a doubling of the mean concentration ratio from 38.8 to 77.6 would result in an advertising-to-sales ratio within the range of 1.0 to 2.2 percent at the 95 percent confidence

---

[17] The generally stronger results in 1967 appear to be due to changes in the composition of the consumer goods subsamples and unusual shifts in advertising intensity for two industries. Because of changes in SIC industry definitions, disclosure problems, and shifts in classification, the following industries were not available for both years: dolls, motor vehicles and parts, morticians' goods, matches, lamp shades, candles, and umbrellas, parasols, and canes. One industry, not elsewhere classified—namely, knitting mills—had a shift in advertising intensity from 1963 to 1967 from 0.06 to 10.59 percent, and a shift in concentration from 34 to 54 percent. Another industry not elsewhere classified—household furniture—had a drop in advertising intensity from 21.67 to 11.19 percent, and a slight rise in concentration from 34 to 36 percent. Thus, as with previous studies, the results appear to be sensitive to the inclusion or exclusion of certain industries.

sumer goods. The situation is similar for producer nondurables (which are material inputs) and producer durables (which are investment or capital goods). Industries were classified according to the percentage of their final output shipped to consumers, the percentage shipped for use as producer material goods, and the percentage shipped for use as investment goods.[16]

The use of four-digit industries, a comprehensive four-digit measure of advertising, a relatively objective method of classifying industries, and larger samples than generally used before should correct for much of the potential measurement error found in previous studies.

The Results

The results for each year for equations (1) and (2) are given in Tables 1, 2, and 3, and those for equations (3) and (4) are given in Tables 4, 5, and 6. Table 1, covering the 1947 sample, shows no significant linear relationship in any subsample, with the exception of consumer durable goods. The most likely subsample for a positive relationship, consumer nondurables, shows no significant relationship. In addition, there is no evidence of an inverted-U or quadratic relationship, casting doubt on the view that advertising intensity decreases at higher levels of concentration. These results are supported by Table 4 where the log of advertising expenditures is used and where no significant relationship is found in any subsample tested. For the 1947 data, there appears to be, in general, no significant relationship between advertising intensity and concentration.

---

[16] Previous studies of four-digit industries have generally based the consumer-producer separation on an unpublished Federal Trade Commission study (see footnote 40, Chapter 1). It classified industries according to the Federal Reserve Board's listing of industries for its production indexes. In contrast, the classification herein is based on the percentage of shipments of output to final demand in four categories: consumption, investment, materials, and government. If 50 percent or more of an industry's output went to consumption, it was classified as a consumer goods industry and if 50 percent or more went to investment plus materials, it was classified as a producer goods industry. When no category had 50 percent or more, as happened occasionally, the industry was classified according to its largest output category. The durable/nondurable producer goods distinction was made by classifying industries with over 50 percent investment shipments as durable and over 50 percent material shipments as nondurable goods categories. For consumer goods, products consumed within a short time (food, beverages, toiletries, cleaners, and certain clothes) were judged nondurable. Durable products were dominated by long-lived household goods such as appliances, furniture, and carpets. The samples tested, along with advertising sales ratios and concentration ratios, are listed in Appendix B.

1963, and 1967.[13] These figures were matched with comparable industry value-of-shipments concentration data in each year.[14] The resulting samples totaled 261, 329, and 324 industries, which composed 58 percent, 79 percent, and 79 percent of all manufacturing industries in 1947, 1963, and 1967 respectively.[15]

Advertising intensity is measured by the inputs purchased by each industry from the advertising sector divided by the value of shipments for that industry (adjusted for imports and secondary output). Advertising input includes talent and production costs, signs and advertising displays, artwork, postage and printing, and media space and time (including newspapers, periodicals, network and spot TV, network and spot radio, outdoor, and motion pictures). Concentration is measured as the ratio of the top four-firm value of shipments to the total industry value of shipments.

The samples in each year were subdivided into consumer, producer, nondurable, and durable goods subsamples in an attempt to hold constant other factors that are likely to affect advertising intensity. Each subsample should provide a group of industries relatively homogeneous in price, frequency of purchase, technological complexity, type of advertising, and type of seller. The type of advertising, price, product complexity, and buying frequency, for example, tend to be more uniform within consumer nondurable goods than for all con-

---

[13] The 1963 and 1967 input–output tables used were the 478 level and 484 level disaggregations, respectively, available on tape from the U.S. Department of Commerce, Office of Business Economics. There was no comparable disaggregation of advertising data available for 1958. The 1947 advertising data is available in a special mimeographed report produced in 1954 entitled *I-O N203 Advertising*, and was generously provided by Philip M. Ritz of the U.S. Department of Commerce.

[14] U.S. Bureau of the Census, Census of Manufactures, 1967, *Special Report Series: Concentration Ratios in Manufacturing*, MC67(s)-2.1 (Washington, D.C.: U.S. Bureau of the Census, 1970); U.S. Congress, Committee on the Judiciary, Subcommittee on Antitrust and Monopoly, "Concentration Ratios in Manufacturing Industry, 1963," 89th Congress, 2nd session, 1966; U.S. Department of Commerce, "Concentration of Industry Report" (Washington, D.C., 1949).

[15] In a prior study on 1963 data alone a sample of 328 industries was used, regressing the advertising/sales ratio on four-firm value-added concentration ratios. The current study differs from the earlier study in that it uses value-of-shipments concentration ratios and reclassifies certain industries into different subsamples based on a more complete treatment of adjusting input–output data for secondary shipments and imports, in order to match Census of Manufactures measures of value of shipments as closely as possible. One industry had no published value-added concentration ratio in 1963 but did have a value-of-shipments ratio, accounting for the difference in total samples. Stanley I. Ornstein, "The Advertising-Concentration Controversy," *Southern Economic Journal*, vol. 43 (July 1976), pp. 892-902.

across all industries is usually highly skewed, with a few industries having very large size values and most industries having relatively much smaller values. Using such data in any least squares estimation tends to make the variance of the error term e nonconstant; that is, the variance of e changes across concentration levels.[11] This violates a basic assumption of the regression model, which is that there are not systematically greater errors for some sets of data than for others. One simple technique for reducing the extent of this error and the bias it may impart is to transform into logarithms the sales and advertising variables. Hence, both sales and advertising are measured in logarithms in equations (3) and (4).

All previous authors who postulated increasing returns to advertising and advertising-created brand loyalty recognized that these presumed barriers to entry would not obtain in all industries. Consequently, they focused almost exclusively on consumer goods industries, reasoning that buyers in producer goods markets are better informed and less easily persuaded by emotional appeals than those in other markets.[12] Advertising is in fact a generally larger fraction of total selling expenditures for consumer goods industries than for producer goods industries. Consumer durable goods, like producer goods, are characterized by relatively high nonadvertising selling expenditures. Thus, the relationships in equations (1) to (4) should be much stronger in consumer than producer goods and in consumer nondurable than consumer durable goods if the conventional hypotheses are valid—that is, if there are increasing returns (economies of scale) in advertising, if advertising creates brand loyalty, and if advertising creates a barrier to entry. For the two alternative hypotheses postulated, the first is most likely to apply to consumer nondurables, and the second is a purely statistical artifact that should apply in both consumer and producer goods industries.

To estimate our equations, advertising data were drawn at the four-digit industry level from the U.S. input-output tables for 1947,

---

[11] The technical term for this error is *heteroscedasticity*. J. Johnston, *Statistical Methods*, pp. 207-211.

[12] There is an explanation of advertising differentials other than that buyers in producer goods markets are less susceptible to emotional appeals—namely, that with fewer buyers in producer goods markets it is not economical to advertise as intensively as in mass consumer goods markets. Promotional expenses are shifted from advertising to direct sales force expenditures in producer goods industries because that is a relatively cheaper means of communicating. Lester G. Telser, "Advertising and the Consumer," *Advertising and Society*, ed. Yale Brozen (New York: New York University Press, 1974), p. 27. For some evidence, see Lambin, *Advertising, Competition, and Conduct*, p. 122.

determined) in most models of industrial structure and performance. In actual practice it makes no difference which variable is dependent or independent in the simple univariate model tested, since the identical statistical results (and hence the identical conclusions) obtain, no matter which variable we start with.

Four equations were estimated:
(1) $ASR = a_1 + b_1 CR + e_1$
(2) $ASR = a_2 + b_2 CR + c_2 CR^2 + e_2$
(3) $\text{Log} A = a_3 + b_3 CR + c_3 \text{Log} S + e_3$
(4) $\text{Log} A = a_4 + b_4 CR + c_4 CR^2 + d_4 \text{Log} S + e_4$

where,

ASR = the industry advertising-to-sales ratio,
CR = the four-firm value-of-shipments concentration ratio,
A = total industry advertising expenditures,
S = total industry sales, and
e = stochastic error term.

Equations (1) and (2) are the usual linear and quadratic equations estimated in previous studies. Although previous studies have not used total advertising as the dependent variable as in equations (3) and (4), this use may be more appropriate than the use of the advertising-to-sales ratio. Much of the theory simply states that there will be more or less advertising, not that there will be higher or lower advertising intensity. Furthermore, the conventional theory on advertising as a barrier to entry implies that the absolute level of advertising expenditures is a more appropriate measure of capital requirements or economies of scale than advertising intensity.[10] The larger the amount spent on advertising, the greater will be the potential economies and the higher the capital requirements (if they exist).

The use of total industry sales and advertising introduces a potential error in the equations. The distribution of such size variables

---

[10] Comanor and Wilson argue that advertising per firm is a better measure of advertising scale economies and absolute capital requirements than advertising/sales ratios for entry at large scale. In contrast to their argument, they find a stronger relationship between industry profit rates and advertising/sales ratios than between profit rates and advertising per firm. Comanor and Wilson, "Advertising, Market Structure, and Performance," p. 428.

Advertising per firm could not be used in the present regressions since concentration and number of firms are tautologically related; that is, high concentration is associated with few firms and low concentration with many firms. Thus advertising per firm and concentration have a spurious positive relationship. Ornstein et al., "Determinants of Market Structure."

In larger sample studies covering IRS industries the opposite results were found. One study of 113 IRS manufacturing industries in 1963 found that mean firm advertising intensity doubled from firms with assets of $500,000 or less (1.2 percent) to those with assets of $50 million or more (2.4 percent). There was also a statistically significant difference in average advertising intensity between the next highest size class ($5 to $50 million—1.9 percent) and the largest size class (2.4 percent).[8] In addition, Comanor and Wilson, using data from forty-one IRS consumer goods industries for 1954–1957, found, on average, that the top four or eight firms had higher advertising intensity than the next four, eight, or twelve firms.[9]

In summary, there are two plausible nontraditional explanations for an observation of a positive relationship between concentration and advertising intensity: (1) where production or distribution scale economies are possible, advertising provides a means of entry into larger markets, leading to increases in firm size (relative to the market size), and thus to higher concentration, and (2) concentration and advertising intensity are spuriously correlated because of large firm effects. The first hypothesis would seem most likely to apply to heavily advertised consumer goods industries, particularly consumer nondurable goods industries which offer frequently purchased, low-priced, experience goods for which advertising serves to identify new brands and product characteristics. The second hypothesis is likely to hold true in both consumer and producer goods markets if large firms advertise more intensively than small firms.

New Models

In principle the interaction effects of advertising and concentration should be tested in a system of simultaneous equations. But, because of the econometric problems involved in such studies, this methodology is not used here. The equations tested adopt a functional form which assumes that concentration explains the level of advertising intensity. This seems sensible, a priori, since advertising as a firm-specific decision variable can hardly be considered exogenous, while concentration is generally considered to be exogenous (that is, pre-

---

[8] Ornstein et al., "Determinants of Market Structure," p. 623.
[9] Comanor and Wilson, *Advertising and Market Power*, pp. 196-216; also see Matityahu Marcus, "The Intensity and Effectiveness of Advertising," *Oxford University Institute of Economics and Statistics*, vol. 32 (November 1970), pp. 339-345.

more efficient firms have a larger margin between price and marginal cost and, according to the Dorfman-Steiner model noted earlier, the higher the price-cost margin the higher will be the optimal advertising intensity. For each of these reasons it may be that, in general, large firms will advertise more intensively than small firms in a given industry.

The average advertising intensity of an industry can be calculated in two ways: (1) by taking the simple average of each firm's advertising-to-sales ratio, and (2) by taking a weighted average by dividing total industry advertising by total industry sales. Almost all studies use the latter method which gives the greater weight to the largest advertisers. If the larger firms have greater advertising-to-sales ratios, then the latter measure will always yield a higher industry average than the former. More important, if an industry's average advertising intensity is dominated by large firms, the influence of large firms on weighted industry average advertising intensity will vary with concentration. Advertising intensity and concentration are thus necessarily positively correlated because of the way advertising intensity is measured.

There is mixed support for the view that higher advertising intensity occurs in the larger firms in a given industry. Reporting on the distribution of advertising intensity in published studies of beer, liquor, and ready-to-eat cereals industries and unpublished data for soap and automobiles, Yale Brozen found that in these industries the smaller firms advertise more intensively than the largest firms.[5] In Lambin's study of 107 brands covering twenty-five Western European product markets, large share brands had smaller advertising intensity on average than small share brands (7.5 percent against 15.9 percent).[6] Reporting on twenty-nine banks in twenty-three distinct metropolitan areas for 1965, Edwards found a negative correlation between a bank's advertising intensity and its individual market share.[7]

---

[5] Ibid., p. 129.

[6] Lambin, *Advertising, Competition, and Conduct*, p. 130.

[7] Franklin R. Edwards, "More on Advertising and Competition in Banking: Reply to Chayim Herzig-Marx," *Antitrust Bulletin*, vol. 21 (Spring 1976), pp. 85-89. These results on banking are instructive, for entry into banking is legally controlled and capitalization for small scale entry is very low. Thus advertising in banking cannot be considered a barrier to small-scale entry but can be viewed as a purely competitive strategy. The results of greater proportionate advertising intensity relative to market share for small market share firms supports the position of Telser, who was one of the first to argue that advertising is a means to entry, is designed to create disloyalty and not loyalty, and leads to market share instability rather than stability.

efficiency of the firm or luck. The beer industry, for example, provides a classic case where economies of scale in production were achieved through advertising-induced shifts in demand, geographic expansion of markets, and changes in production technology.[2] Studies of the effects of advertising on the price, cost, and market structure for eyeglasses and for toys show that advertising can replace local monopolists with high-volume, low-cost, lower-priced competitors.[3] For eyeglasses, the introduction of advertising made possible an increase in the geographic area over which buyers could be informed, allowing production and distribution economies of scale. For toys, the establishment of brand identification made price comparisons easy for retail shoppers, increased sales volume, and lowered retail costs. To be sure, examples of this sort are rare in recent times, since advertising has been established for quite a while in most industries, but these examples are indicative—not least because they suggest that increased concentration may have little or no connection with advertising barriers to entry.[4]

One further explanation for the apparent relationship between advertising and concentration is that it is only apparent—that is, purely a statistical phenomenon. Large firms may have both greater total advertising expenditures and greater intensity than smaller firms within an industry. The larger firms have the larger markets to serve. They require wider exposure and more repetition in their advertising because they face a larger turnover of buyers. In addition, they may have a rate of new product introduction higher than for small firms, indicating a younger mix of products and a need for greater advertising intensity. Lastly, large firms tend to grow large because they offer superior quality per unit price. Since the probability of repeat sales increases with higher product quality, then holding price constant, advertising is more effective for high than for low-quality producers, and for large rather than small firms. The

---

[2] Donald A. Norman, "Structural Change and Performance in the U.S. Brewing Industry," doctoral dissertation, University of California, Los Angeles, 1975.

[3] Lee Benham, "The Effect of Advertising on the Price of Eyeglasses," *Journal of Law and Economics*, vol. 15 (October 1972), pp. 337-352; Robert Steiner, "Does Advertising Lower Consumer Prices?" *Journal of Marketing*, vol. 37 (October 1973), pp. 19-26.

[4] It may be argued the resulting increase in concentration worsens allocative efficiency if marginal cost falls more than price. However, a lower price means buyers are better off than facing a higher price and a smaller price-cost margin. Yale Brozen, "Entry Barriers: Advertising and Product Differentiation," *Industrial Concentration: The New Learning*, Harvey J. Goldschmid, H. Michael Mann, and J. Fred Weston, eds. (Boston: Little, Brown, 1974), pp. 121-122, note 30.

3
NEW FINDINGS

Given little support for a positive relationship between advertising intensity and concentration based on traditional arguments of scale economies and brand loyalty, are there alternative explanations for a positive relationship? One is the view described above that nonprice competition is potentially more profitable than price competition in highly concentrated industries. At least two additional explanations can be postulated.

Advertising, as a source of information, serves as a prerequisite for expanded firm output, especially for local and regional firms seeking larger geographic markets. By providing information, advertising may lead to shifts in demand and in the elasticity of demand. Production increases or changes in distribution methods to serve increased demand may lead to cost reductions through economies of scale in manufacturing or distribution. The result will be increased concentration (assuming the optimum size of the firms increases more than the size of the market). The newly enlarged firms will maintain their high levels of advertising intensity.

More generally, advertising—along with luck, managerial skill, and successful research and development—may lead to different growth rates across firms and thus changes in concentration without a direct causal link.[1] That is, increases in advertising may be related to increases in concentration simply because both derive from the firm's underlying growth path, and both increases are related to the

---

[1] For an explanation and evidence of the process by which chance can lead to a positive relationship between advertising intensity and concentration, see Richard B. Mancke, "Causes of Interfirm Profitability Difference: A New Interpretation of the Evidence," *Quarterly Journal of Economics*, vol. 88 (May 1974), pp. 181-193. Also, see Yale Brozen's foreword to Kenneth Clarkson, *Intangible Capital and Rates of Return* (Washington, D.C.: American Enterprise Institute, 1977).

cal evidence is conflicting and does not clarify the contradictory theories. A survey of twenty-three previous studies in Appendix A shows that the studies obtain significant or insignificant results with approximately equal frequency. There seems to be little clear support for the notion that advertising is either a source or a consequence of monopoly power.

General agreement is possible, however, on the *lack* of any clear evidence or theory. First, there is a general lack of empirical support for existing theories of economies of scale in advertising and little evidence of advertising-created brand loyalty. Second, the direction of causality, if any exists, is in doubt, a fact that causes any single equation estimate to be biased. Third, most studies have been plagued by potentially large measurement error and the use of small samples highly sensitive to the inclusion or exclusion of one or two industries.

However, selection of samples can be improved and measurement errors reduced substantially. This is the subject of the next chapter and the ensuing statistical tests.

Summary

The case for the inverted-U or quadratic relationship—where concentration and advertising intensity are positively related up to some intermediate level of concentration and negatively related thereafter—is weak. Academic theorists have not, in fact, agreed that advertising and concentration are positively or negatively related in highly concentrated industries. More important, the samples tested so far are small (for the most part) and subject to bias through the inclusion or exclusion of particular industries. Most important, the quadratic form of the estimating equation is not consistent with the theory advanced to support it.

The studies using simultaneous equations have likewise left something to be desired. Greer's difficulties have been noted above (p. 31)—among them the small size of his sample. The Strickland-Weiss estimates use a sample larger than Greer's, but are subject to a different problem. Of the 417 four-digit industries in the 1963 Census of Manufactures, only 230 exactly match the input-output sectors from which advertising-to-shipments ratios were computed. As a result, the advertising-to-shipments ratios were averages of two or more four-digit industries for fully 44 percent of their industries. This method could introduce large errors in measuring advertising-sales ratios and bias their results.[30]

In general, use of the two-stage least squares technique has given results little different from those given by ordinary least squares. Thus, the initial hope that simultaneous equation models would help resolve the issues has been largely disappointed.

The meaning of the investigations summarized here is uncertain and, as a result, makes them a poor guide toward public policy on advertising as a source of monopoly power. The theories are contradictory, suggesting positive, negative, and no relationship. The empiri-

---

[30] An example of the type of error introduced by this procedure can be illustrated with the drug industry. The census includes three four-digit industries under the broader three-digit drug industry while the input-output tables list only the three-digit drug industry. In the census, "drugs" comprise biological products (bacterial and virus vaccines, toxoids, and blood derivatives), medicinal chemicals and botanicals (bulk manufacturing of basic ground products, basic vitamins, and endocrine products), and pharmaceutical preparations (primarily prescription and over-the-counter drugs). Clearly, advertising intensity varies widely across these industries with large advertising expenditures in pharmaceutical preparations and much lower expenditures in the other two. Yet Strickland and Weiss treat these industries as if they were identical, using the same ratio of advertising-sales (from the input-output sector for drugs) for each separate four-digit industry.

input-output data to compute advertising-to-sales ratios for 408 SIC four-digit industries, have found evidence of both a linear and a quadratic relationship—a relationship that, as might be expected, is stronger for consumer goods industries than for producer goods industries.[27] Using both ordinary least squares and two-stage least squares estimation methods, they find that concentration is positively and significantly related to advertising intensity and economies of scale (measured by a proxy for minimum efficient scale of plant), with the ordinary least squares equation explaining almost 50 percent of the variation in concentration. They conclude that advertising increases with concentration and that advertising leads to higher concentration because of substantial advertising scale economies; however, they present no evidence of such scale economies.

The best theoretical basis for a simultaneous equation model (and one used in the Strickland-Weiss study) has been offered by Richard Schmalensee, who concludes that the optimal advertising-to-sales ratio is determined by three factors: (1) margin between price and marginal cost, (2) the expected response of competitors to a firm's advertising strategy, and (3) the advertising elasticity of demand facing the firm and its competitors.[28] If marginal cost is constant and if the sum of the last two factors (which is the net advertising elasticity of demand) is constant, then price and advertising must be directly related—that is, advertising rises with price and price rises with advertising. Similarly, profits as a percentage of sales rise with price, and under profit-maximizing conditions there must be a positive correlation between advertising intensity and profitability, *even when advertising is independent of monopoly power*. If this is true, any single equation model must yield meaningless results, inasmuch as any increase in prices would raise both advertising intensity and profit margins. Moreover, if concentration is positively related to profitability, it must necessarily be related to advertising intensity, though no causal relationship would exist between the two. It should be noted here that, using ordinary least squares, Strickland and Weiss found a significant positive relationship between advertising and profit margins but that their two-stage least squares equations show insignificant or barely significant relationships.[29] However, concentration and advertising intensity were positively related using both estimation techniques.

---

[27] Allyn Strickland and Leonard W. Weiss, "Advertising, Concentration, and Price-Cost Margins," *Journal of Political Economy*, October 1976, pp. 1109-1121.
[28] Schmalensee, *The Economics of Advertising*, pp. 222-226.
[29] Strickland and Weiss, "Advertising, Concentration, and Price-Cost Margins," pp. 1116-1118.

he failed to take into account the different characteristics of product supply and demand among the twenty-five industries.[24] He subdivided a sample of sixty-three consumer nondurable goods markets into four categories—foodstuffs, toiletries, kitchen and household supplies, and medicaments—and found no evidence for linear or quadratic relationships either within any subsample or overall. R. D. Rees criticized Sutton for failing to recognize the potential bias from two-way causality, for introducing biases into data by including excise taxes and by his way of constructing concentration ratios, and for failing to appreciate the advantages of nonprice competition in highly concentrated industries.[25] Retesting after making corrections for these errors, Rees found no significant quadratic relationships among the data.

Two recent studies offer further conflicting evidence on possible quadratic relationships between advertising and concentration. Using trade journal data for the late 1950s, Brian Brush has calculated advertising-to-sales ratios for twenty-eight consumer goods industries for the United States.[26] Brush adopts the sampling method of Mann, Henning, and Meehan by assigning firms to individual industries, using two to four firms per industry to construct weighted average industry advertising-sales ratios. His tests are thus subject to the same statistical problems as Mann, Henning, and Meehan's studies, as noted above (p. 18). Taking concentration, rate of industry growth, market size, and product durability as independent variables, Brush finds support for a positive linear relationship but not for a quadratic relationship between advertising intensity and concentration. Allyn Strickland and Leonard Weiss, on the other hand, using 1963 U.S.

---

[24] W. Duncan Reekie, "Advertising and Market Structure: Another Approach," *Economic Journal*, vol. 85 (March 1975), pp. 156-164. Some doubt exists as to the validity of Reekie's study since he used brand share data based on consumer-recall surveys for measures of concentration. Such surveys frequently are highly inaccurate.

[25] R. D. Rees, "Advertising, Concentration, and Competition: A Comment and Further Results," *Economic Journal*, vol. 85 (March 1975), pp. 165-174. It appears that Sutton's theory is even more vulnerable to critical analysis. For example, his theory is crucially dependent on an assumed relationship between concentration and the size distribution of firms, and differences in firm size between entrants and existing firms. He provides no evidence on either assumption. In contrast to his claims, economic theory states that concentration levels are a function of firm size relative to market size, so that small markets may have high concentration and small firms, while large markets may have low concentration and large firms. Further, there is nothing which prevents new entrants from being large relative to existing firms.

[26] Brian Brush, "The Influence of Market Structure on Industry Advertising Intensity," *Journal of Industrial Economics*, September 1976, pp. 55-67.

advertise. Gains at the expense of rivals are thought to be greatest when there are large differences in sales or resources among competing firms as a result of economies of scale in advertising. (It will be remembered that such scale economies have little empirical support.) Sutton believes that economies of scale result from the indivisibility of advertising and from the advertising price structures imposed by the media (both of these being dubious).[23] In his view, the requisite dispersion in firm size is most likely in moderately concentrated industries, whereas in highly concentrated industries collusion on advertising is likely.

If higher total profits are a result of improved profit margins, the role played by advertising, according to Sutton, is to preserve high profits by erecting barriers to entry. Sutton invokes the size distribution of firms as a proxy for barriers to entry. In unconcentrated industries, he states, new entrants and existing firms will be roughly the same size, and any entry barriers attributable to advertising will be low. Likewise, in highly concentrated industries, collusion will raise firm profit margins to the point that they cannot be further raised (except for a firm that cheats without being detected). However, in moderately concentrated industries, Sutton assumes new firms will be much smaller than existing firms, and the advertising economies of scale will create barriers to entry. Sutton's conclusion is that advertising intensity increases up to moderate levels of concentration and then decreases. In other words, he specified a theoretical model to explain the inverted-U or quadratic relationship. It will be noted that the explanatory power of this model depends on the existence of economies of scale in advertising and a particular size distribution of firms in various concentration ranges.

Sutton's empirical work showed no support for a linear model of the relationship between advertising and concentration. What he did was to regress advertising intensity on five-firm concentration for twenty-five British consumer goods industries in 1963. Although the linear model was insignificant, the quadratic model "explained" 34 percent of the variation in advertising. Advertising sales reached a maximum level of 2.9 percent when five-firm concentration reached 63.8 percent. Sutton also calculated regression equations for fourteen producer goods industries, finding no significant statistical relationship. There is, however, a question—indeed, there are several questions—to be raised on his statistical techniques.

W. Duncan Reekie criticized Sutton's work on the grounds that

---

[23] See above, pp. 10-12.

such characteristics as product complexity, advertising media, and buyer turnover, and their effects on advertising intensity.

The two dependent variables used were advertising to sales (specifically the 1963 ratio of major media advertising expenses to sales) and the (estimated) stock of advertising capital to sales. These were related to (regressed on) seller concentration (measured by the "Herfindahl index"[21] and by the three-firm concentration ratio), total sales, a dummy variable reflecting sensitive psychological drives (the markets being lipstick, toothpaste, toilet soap, and face powder), number of brands, the 1963 ratio of new brands to existing brands, sales growth from 1958 to 1963, and income elasticity in 1963. The results show a significant quadratic relationship between advertising and the Herfindahl concentration index and a significant linear (but not quadratic) relationship when concentration is measured by the three-firm ratio. The regressions explain about 50 percent of the variation in advertising intensity.

C. J. Sutton has noted that the inconsistent results from tests of a linear relationship may result from the fact that the true relationship is nonlinear.[22] He attempted to outline a theory for a nonlinear relationship by showing how the incentive and opportunity for advertising are affected by market structure or concentration. He assumes that advertising will vary directly with the expected value of the increase in profits it will produce. The increase in profits will come either from an increase in sales or from an improvement in profit margins. Sales increases will come either from increases in overall industry sales (with the firm getting the same percentage share of larger market sales) or at the expense of rival firms (a larger share of the same market) or possibly both (a larger share of a larger market). In unconcentrated industries, Sutton argues, firms are unlikely to advertise so as to increase industry sales—they are much more likely to try to "ride free" on the advertising of others, if others

---

[21] The Herfindahl index is another measure of industry concentration. It is measured by calculating the market share of each firm in an industry, and then summing the squared values of each firm's market share. Algebraically, it is
$$HI = \sum_{i=1}^{n} (s_i)^2,$$
where s_i equals share of ith firm and n equals the total number of firms in an industry. This index is more inclusive than the traditional four-firm concentration since it is affected by both the total number of firms and the size distribution over all firms. However, it is seldom used in the United States since the market share of each firm in an industry is rarely available to the public. For a more complete discussion of concentration ratios, see Stigler, *The Organization of Industry*, pp. 29-38.

[22] Sutton, "Advertising, Concentration, and Competition," pp. 56-69.

bility of Cable's attack, his own results are ambiguous and not particularly useful.

Beginning with the rules for optimal advertising intensity developed for static conditions by Dorfman and Steiner and for dynamic conditions by Nerlove and Arrow, Cable attempted to show that any relationship between concentration and advertising intensity must be a function of price elasticity and advertising elasticity of demand.[19] The Dorfman-Steiner theorem implies that a profit-maximizing firm will adjust the ratio of advertising to sales until it equals the ratio of advertising elasticity of demand to (the absolute value of) the price elasticity of demand. As price elasticity falls, therefore, with advertising elasticity constant, the optimal advertising-to-sales ratio rises. If a decrease in the number of firms in an industry (an increase in concentration) decreases the number of available substitute goods and produces lower price elasticity for the individual firm, then optimal advertising intensity should rise, unless offset by changes in advertising elasticity of demand.

The link between advertising and concentration through price and advertising elasticities is complex and quite tenuous, to say the least. The presumed negative relationship between concentration and price elasticity depends on how firms react to each other's pricing policies and on the degree of product homogeneity. Since these reactions are generally complex and unknown, a simple negative relationship is more an act of faith than a theoretical deduction. In addition, when price interaction effects are considered, the results are ambiguous, depending as they do on a firm's own and its rivals' advertising strategies and the costs of collusion. In Cable's words, "There is strictly no unequivocal theoretical prediction about the relationship between advertising and concentration."[20]

Nevertheless, Cable does suggest that collusion may lead to an inverted-U or quadratic relationship between advertising and concentration. He tests for such a relationship, using twenty-six narrowly defined United Kingdom nondurable consumer goods (for example, instant coffee, lipstick, and baked beans). The industries were selected to be largely alike in price of product, frequency of purchase, and the kind of retail outlet where the product is sold. The purpose of this selection is to reduce intermarket differences in

---

[19] Robert Dorfman and Peter O. Steiner, "Optimal Advertising and Optimal Quality," *American Economic Review*, vol. 44 (December 1954), pp. 820-836; Marc Nerlove and Kenneth J. Arrow, "Optimal Advertising Policy under Dynamic Conditions," *Economica*, vol. 29 (May 1962), pp. 129-142.

[20] Cable, "Market Structure and Advertising Intensity," p. 112.

single equation estimates when there is two-way causality. Unfortunately, Greer's results were mixed, and he was unable to say anything about the extent of bias in his single equation ordinary least squares regression estimates.

The dependent variables used by Greer in his simultaneous equation estimates are advertising intensity, concentration, and the growth rate of sales. His independent variables include relative price change, income elasticity, economies of scale, and capital barriers to entry.[15] His results are at best mixed, with advertising appearing as a statistically significant determinant of concentration for some tests and for some product classes, but not for others, and with concentration appearing as a statistically significant determinant of advertising for some tests and for some product classes, but not for others. By Greer's admission, there are errors in the manner in which his equations were specified. Moreover, there is a problem of multicollinearity (the independent variables may not in fact be independent of each other), which biases the results, making interpretation of each variable questionable. And above and beyond this, the small sample sizes call into question the efficiency of the two-stage least squares approach. Despite these problems, he concludes that "advertising has been a very important determinant of market structure in these industries and, conversely, structure a determinant of advertising."[16]

Mann, Henning, and Meehan reestimated the ordinary least squares relationship, dropping one industry from each class, and found the squared concentration coefficient to be insignificant in six out of nine cases.[17] John Cable has attacked the use of ordinary least squares regressions, charging that studies not based on assumed structural relationships among the variables will omit variables and leave questions of definition substantially unresolved (why, for example, is advertising to sales the proper measure of advertising intensity?), in addition to making unprovable assumptions of linearity and ignoring the direction of cause and effect.[18] Despite the plausi-

---

[15] Economies of scale are measured as average plant size among plants accounting for the top 50 percent of sales as a percentage of total market sales. Algebraically this is expressed as $S/2n/S = 1/2n$, where S equals industry sales and n equals the number of plants accounting for the top 50 percent of sales. Capital requirements are calculated as average plant size, $S/2n$, times the ratio of total assets to total sales for an industry. Comanor and Wilson, "Advertising, Market Structure, and Performance," pp. 428-429.

[16] Greer, "Advertising and Market Concentration," p. 32.

[17] H. M. Mann, J. A. Henning, and J. W. Meehan, Jr., "Advertising and Market Concentration: Comment," *Southern Economic Journal*, vol. 39 (January 1973), pp. 448-451.

[18] Cable, "Market Structure and Advertising Intensity," pp. 105-124.

rather than the other way around. Finally, at high levels of concentration, the relationship becomes negative: increases in concentration yield decreases in advertising intensity through collusion, and advertising may allow successful new entry, yielding decreases in concentration. In short, advertising and concentration are "interacting in cause and effect over time, frequently simultaneously determining the historical result."[14]

Greer attempted to test this hypothesis with the IRS samples used by Telser. He divided the samples into three classes in order to account for the differences in advertising that are brought about by product characteristics. In ascending order of assumed relative advertising profitability, these classes are: (1) frequently purchased standard convenience goods, (2) infrequently purchased luxury goods, and (3) moderately priced specialty convenience goods. Greer estimated the relationship between concentration (the independent variable) and advertising (the dependent variable) in quadratic form, with sales growth as a second independent variable for each product class and for all classes, in 1948, 1954, and 1957. Sales growth was generally insignificant, while concentration and the square of concentration were significant for the first two classes each year. They were not significant for the third class or for all classes taken together.

Because the use of single equations might produce a seriously flawed result if indeed there were two-way causality, Greer estimated simultaneous equations in two ways to test for the seriousness of "simultaneous equation bias." In order to do this, he organized his variables into different sets of "structural equations." (A structural equation is supposed to show the underlying behavioral relationship that links one dependent variable with some, though not necessarily all, of the independent variables and with other dependent variables in an economic system.) Then, in one test, he simply estimated these equations one at a time in order to see how much of the variation in each dependent variable could be explained by each equation (this is the ordinary least squares estimation process). In the second test, he rearranged his original, structural equations in order to estimate each of the dependent variables in terms of all the independent variables, and then he used the estimated values of the dependent variables to estimate each of the original equations (this is the two-stage least squares estimation process).

A comparison of the ordinary least squares and two-stage least squares results will, in theory, show the extent of error in using

---

[14] Ibid., p. 23.

collusion. Indeed, according to Scherer, fear of being left behind creates an incentive for rivals to engage in excessive advertising—that is, advertising beyond the level that maximizes joint profits. Citing historical evidence, he finds "that oligopolies often fail to coordinate their advertising policies successfully, spending much more than they would under joint profit maximization."[11] In addition, it has been suggested by Julian Simon that advertising collusion is basically unstable (1) because variations in promotional expenditures within a given accounting period are hard to detect and (2) because promotional expenditure levels cannot be changed quickly—a point echoing Scherer's view on the time lag inherent in responding to a rival's "cheating" against the colluders.[12]

Review of Major Studies

Douglas Greer was one of the first scholars to recognize and stress the possibility of a nonlinear relationship between advertising and concentration, as well as the possibility of two-way causality—that is, of an interaction between advertising and concentration, with each supporting (or even causing) the other.[13] Greer argued that the hypothesis of a linear relationship was unrealistic once a sufficiently high range of concentration was reached (1) because in that range of concentration there would be decreasing returns to advertising and (2) because in that range of concentration there would be collusion on advertising. He suggested that there would be a positive correlation between the two variables when the four largest firms in an industry control less than 50 percent of the market. In the middle range of concentration there is overinvestment in advertising owing to advertising "warfare." At higher levels of concentration, collusion takes place and advertising intensity decreases to the joint-profit-maximizing level.

Greer held that at low levels of concentration a rise in advertising intensity causes a rise in concentration, as a result of economies of scale in advertising, the greater financial resources of large firms, and differential rates of advertising success among firms. At moderate levels of concentration, however, the direction of causality is reversed as advertising competition becomes superior to price competition: increases in concentration cause increases in advertising intensity,

---

[11] Ibid., p. 336.
[12] Simon, *Issues in the Economics of Advertising*, pp. 106-107.
[13] Greer, "Advertising and Market Concentration," pp. 19-32.

tries would have an incentive to choose nonprice rather than price competition.

On the other hand, some scholars—Greer, Cable, and Sutton, for example—believe that high degrees of concentration are likely to be accompanied by advertising collusion.[6] Whether collusion is likely or not depends on the costs and benefits of collusion. Stigler's theory of oligopoly assumes that, in order to maximize profits, firms always seek to collude on price.[7] Whether an agreement will be stable or not depends on the costs of monitoring price cheaters and the costs of enforcing agreements, since there are always gains for an individual firm that cheats. But the same logic can be applied to nonprice variables such as advertising. If it is the difficulty of policing that determines the stability of collusion, then indeed collusion is more likely on advertising (which is highly visible and therefore easily policed) than on price competition (where rebates or price cuts may be hidden).[8] Stigler's argument here is accepted by James Ferguson, who notes (1) that monitoring is easy, since there are independent advertising-reporting services that monitor brand and firm advertising and report to rival sellers, and (2) that firms are always preparing new advertising campaigns and can initiate them at a moment's notice should a rival decide to cheat.[9]

Others disagree, maintaining that collusion on advertising is more difficult than collusion on price. According to Frederic Scherer, "Any fool can match a price cut, but counteracting a clever advertising gambit is far from easy."[10] For one thing, price cuts can be matched almost immediately, but a retaliatory advertising campaign may take weeks or months to plan and carry out. The resulting lag gives the advertiser with a head start time to earn large profits at his rivals' expense and, therefore, an incentive to cheat against advertising

---

[6] See above, note 1.

[7] George J. Stigler, "A Theory of Oligopoly," *Journal of Political Economy*, vol. 72 (February 1964), pp. 44-61.

[8] This is partially contradicted by Stigler's theory of oligopoly and some independent evidence. Stigler's oligopoly model predicts that price competition will increase as market share instability increases. Telser and Reekie found that market share instability increased with advertising intensity, which they conclude is evidence that advertising leads to greater competition. If advertising intensity and concentration are positively related, then the probability of price collusion is reduced under the Stigler model at high levels of concentration. Telser, "Advertising and Competition," p. 548; Reekie, "Advertising and Market Share Mobility," pp. 143-158.

[9] Ferguson, *Advertising and Concentration*, p. 26.

[10] Frederic M. Scherer, *Industrial Market Structure and Economic Performance* (Chicago: Rand McNally, 1970), p. 335.

depend on the empirical proposition that the marginal cost of advertising is rising and that it is rising faster than the marginal cost of production.

Stigler's argument applies, of course, to a special situation—a cartel with particular types of cost curves. Consistent with his argument, most empirical studies do in fact support the assumption that there are diminishing returns to advertising (or that the cost of selling an additional unit by advertising becomes higher and higher as advertising rises) and that there are constant returns to production (or that the cost of producing, as opposed to advertising, an additional unit at some point becomes constant).[3] It would therefore appear that at least some of the assumptions underlying one argument that advertising is caused by, rather than a cause of, concentration are satisfied. There may, of course, be other reasons why advertising expenditures may be expected to be higher in industries where there is substantial concentration than they are in industries with many more firms. Let us look briefly at some of these.

First, any advertising-induced shift in industry demand probably raises the sales of all the firms in that industry. The larger the firm's initial market share, the greater its probable gain from new sales and the greater its incentive to advertise relative to small share firms in low-concentration industries. Second, price competition is less likely in those industries whose firms face price-inelastic demands than in those industries whose firms face price-elastic demands—if lowering prices does not increase sales appreciably, why lower prices? Sales gains from price competition in industries with inelastic demands come mainly at the expense of rivals and do not lead to appreciable increases in industry demand. On the other hand, competition through advertising not only should transfer sales across firms but also should increase industry sales generally.[4] Whether demand is relatively price-inelastic in highly concentrated industries is an empirical question whose answer has not yet been determined, although firms in highly concentrated industries are generally thought to face more price-inelastic demands.[5] If they do, then highly concentrated indus-

---

[3] Lambin, *Advertising, Competition, and Market Conduct*, pp. 95-98; A. A. Walters, "An Econometric Survey of Production and Cost Functions," *Econometrica*, vol. 31 (January-April 1963), pp. 1-66.

[4] Lester G. Telser, "How Much Does It Pay Whom to Advertise?" *American Economic Review*, vol. 50 (May 1961), pp. 194-205.

[5] George J. Stigler, *The Theory of Price* (New York: Macmillan Co., 1966), pp. 90, 342. For an alternative point of view, see Eugene F. Fama and Arthur B. Laffer, "The Number of Firms and Competition," *American Economic Review*, vol. 62 (September 1972), pp. 670-674.

creases advertising intensity, and then reviews individual studies estimating the quadratic relation and simultaneous equation models.

Advertising and the Behavior of Oligopolies

If we are to determine whether the relationship between advertising and concentration turns negative at high levels of concentration, we must look at the behavior of firms under conditions of interdependence. Some economists contend that nonprice competition (product improvement, consumer service, advertising) is more likely under oligopoly than under low concentration conditions. Others contend that high concentration will produce collusion to restrict advertising. First, the argument that nonprice competition is more prevalent under oligopoly is discussed.

Economists traditionally argue that nonprice competition is more profitable than price competition in oligopolistic industries—their underlying assumption being that changes in nonprice competition are not as easily matched by rivals as are changes in price. George Stigler has analyzed this argument within the framework of a cartel which is faced with two choices: whether to collude on advertising (taking advertising as the prototype of nonprice competition) and allow price competition or to collude on price and compete by advertising.[2] Under the first choice, if marginal costs (including advertising) rise with output, price competition will not eliminate profits. The increase in output brought about by price competition will not cause price to fall as much as the industry's collusion on advertising will cause marginal costs to fall. However, if marginal costs do not rise with output, firms will expand output until price has fallen by as much as marginal costs have fallen, and profits will be eliminated. Under the second choice (collusion on price and competition in advertising), profits will again be present if marginal costs are rising. The faster the marginal costs of advertising rise relative to the marginal cost of production the greater the profits. However, if marginal costs are constant, firms will expand output by advertising, competing until the costs of advertising reduce profits to zero. Thus, under either possibility profits may be zero, depending on the marginal cost of advertising. The notion that nonprice competition is more effective in preserving profits in a cartel than price competition is seen to

---

[2] George J. Stigler, "Price and Nonprice Competition," *The Organization of Industry* (Homewood, Ill.: Richard D. Irwin, 1968), pp. 23-28.

2
DOES CONCENTRATION CAUSE INCREASED ADVERTISING?

In the early 1970s there occurred a fundamental shift in academic thinking on the relationship between advertising and industrial concentration, with cause and effect changing places: whereas it had been argued that advertising causes increased concentration, it was now argued that concentration causes increased advertising—or else that causality runs both ways. Moreover, new attention was paid to the possibility that the mixed results of earlier studies might have had their origins in the assumption of a linear relationship when the true relationship between the variables was nonlinear. In this connection, an attempt to provide a theoretical rationale for Kaldor and Silverman's inverted-U or quadratic relationship between advertising and concentration was made. Studies by Greer, Cable, and Sutton suggested that Kaldor's (and Bain's) reasons for expecting a positive relationship between advertising and concentration were valid up to an intermediate level of concentration but that, at very high concentration, a negative relationship existed owing primarily to collusion on advertising.[1]

If the true relationship between advertising and concentration is in fact nonlinear, then (as we noted in Chapter 1) new equations will have to be used to test for the relationship. If causality runs both ways, then these new equations will have to be a set of simultaneous equations. This chapter examines arguments that concentration in-

---

[1] Douglas F. Greer, "Advertising and Market Concentration," *Southern Economic Journal*, vol. 38 (July 1971), pp. 19-32; John Cable, "Market Structure, Advertising Policy, and Intermarket Differences in Advertising Intensity," *Market Structure and Corporate Behavior*, ed. Keith Cowling (London: Gray-Mills Publishing, Ltd., 1972), pp. 105-124; C. J. Sutton, "Advertising, Concentration, and Competition," *Economic Journal*, vol. 84 (March 1974), pp. 56-69.

and low product differentiation. It should also be noted that, even if all these difficulties were not present, the language of the conclusions is not supported by the statistical findings.

Summary

There is practically no support for the Kaldor-Bain view that advertising causes high concentration because of scale economies in advertising and brand loyalty as a capital barrier to entry. There is no evidence of substantial scale economies or of a relation between brand loyalty and advertising. The results of studies looking directly at advertising and concentration are uncertain at best. Moreover, we will see in Chapter 2 that even if a positive relationship exists it by no means is evidence of monopoly power. Given this record of findings, it remains a puzzle why the Kaldor-Bain view continues to dominate economic thought.

Willard Mueller and Larry Hamm used the same data, extended to 1970, to investigate mean changes in concentration.[44] Like Marcus, they found a greater increase in consumer than in producer goods industries and the largest increase in the "high product differentiation" industries. In their study, size of industry and net firm entry were also included as explanatory variables. Regressions were run for all comparable industries for 1947–1970, 1947–1958, and 1958–1970, with high and medium product differentiation coming out positively related to concentration changes and low differentiation insignificantly related in 1947–1958 but significantly positive in the next period. The initial year's concentration was significant (which of course means only that those industries already concentrated cannot increase their concentration as much as those not), while the other "explanatory" factors yield mixed results. The conclusion is that "product differentiation exerted a powerful positive influence on concentration trends over the 23-year period 1947–1970."[45]

The data, as noted, are subject to internal inconsistencies in their definition. For example (as shown by the 1963 input-output tables), flavorings and syrups (61 percent of output shipped to producers) and watchcases (94 percent of output shipped to producers) are misclassified as "consumer goods," while among the firms classified as having high product differentiation (an advertising-to-sales ratio "substantially" over 1 percent) are those in the chocolate and cocoa products industry (1.1 percent), the flavorings industry (1.3 percent), knit outerwear mills (0.6 percent), knit underwear mills (0.4 percent), greeting card manufacturers (0.5 percent), shoe manufacturers (1.0 percent), storage batteries firms (0.4 percent), automobile manufacturers (0.6 percent), and the watchcase manufacturers (0.7 percent). On the other hand, manufacturers of ophthalmic products (3.6 percent) and jewelry (3.1 percent) were classified as low product differentiation firms.

The results of these studies are dependent on their classification of industries. This classification is largely specious because of inconsistencies in classifying industries, examination of only the slowest growing and least technologically dynamic industries, incomplete and ill-defined connections between advertising intensity and product differentiation, and use of largely arbitrary categories of high, medium,

---

[44] Willard F. Mueller and Larry G. Hamm, "Trends in Industrial Market Concentration, 1947 to 1970," *Review of Economics and Statistics*, vol. 56 (November 1974), pp. 511-520.
[45] Ibid., p. 519.

such a multidimensioned concept as product differentiation was not explained. The data are subject to internal inconsistencies in definition, as noted below.[41]

Matityahu Marcus, using this set of data, regressed changes in eight-firm concentration on two dummy variables representing high and medium differentiation.[42] (The number 1 was assigned to each of the dummy variables if the industry fell into that category; 0 was assigned if it did not.) Marcus also included the growth rate for each industry and the initial year's level of concentration, arguing that rapidly growing industries should show decreases in concentration because of the inability of large firms to grow as fast as small firms and that concentrated industries should show declines in concentration as large firms deliberately give up market share to smaller firms. He ran regressions for seventy-eight consumer goods industries for 1947–1963, 1954–1963, and 1958–1963. All three test periods showed the expected (positive) relationships between changes in concentration and the dummy variables. Growth rate and initial year concentration were inversely related in each period. For the period as a whole, concentration increased substantially for highly differentiated product industries, it increased less for those with medium differentiation, and it decreased slightly for low differentiation consumer goods and for producer goods industries. Marcus concluded that "advertising can be expected to lead to [a] substantial rise in industry concentration."[43]

---

[41] For a more complete critique of this data set and the studies based on it, see Stanley I. Ornstein and Steven Lustgarten, "Advertising Intensity and Industrial Concentration: An Empirical Inquiry, 1947 to 1970," in *Issues in Advertising: The Economics of Persuasion* (Washington, D.C.: American Enterprise Institute, forthcoming).

[42] Matityahu Marcus, "Advertising and Changes in Concentration," *Southern Economic Journal*, vol. 36 (October 1969), pp. 117-121.

[43] Ibid., p. 121. David J. Theroux, "Marcus's 'Advertising in Concentration'" (unpublished term paper, University of Chicago Graduate School of Business, 1976) finds that when the FTC industries examined by Marcus are reclassified into "high," "medium," and "low" differentiation categories, according to the input-output advertising data used in this study, the observed positive advertising-concentration relationship virtually disappears. The reclassification of his industries causes Marcus's model to explain a far smaller fraction of the variance in concentration (sometimes none of the variance) than it previously explained. Also, the reclassification upsets the order and direction of the impact of advertising on concentration: "high" and "medium" differentiation no longer exert a uniformly positive impact on concentration and almost never exceed the impact of "low" differentiation. The reclassified Marcus "high" differentiation group shows a smaller increase in concentration over 1947 to 1962 than the original; the reclassified "medium" differentiation groups occasionally show smaller concentration ratios than the reclassified "low" differentiation groups; and the spread between reclassified "high" and "low" differentiation concentration ratios is lower than the original. These findings are reinforced when the corrected Marcus model is tested for four-firm concentration and when the industries examined in this study are substituted for his.

metropolitan areas.[38] His index of concentration was a ratio of deposits in the three largest banks in the area to the total deposits in the area, and he took advertising expenditures from a special survey of the fifty largest national banks in 1965. Even when proxy variables were included to try to take economies of scale and market growth into account, the results showed no significant relationship between concentration and advertising intensity.

Changes in Concentration and Advertising Intensity. A number of studies have attempted to test Kaldor's hypothesis that increases in advertising produce increases in concentration, some by tests for correlation between changes in the two variables and some by tests for correlation between levels of advertising intensity and changes in concentration. The first set of studies, using IRS data for 1947–1963 and various subperiods therein, found no significant relationship between the changes in the two variables.[39] This would appear to contradict Kaldor's hypothesis. The second set, using Federal Trade Commission classifications of four-digit SIC industries into producer and consumer goods industries with high, medium, and low degrees of product differentiation, found significant correlations between product differentiation classes and concentration—though for reasons which will shortly be made clear, it is doubtful that the data used are good enough to support their conclusions.

The sample used in these tests consists of 213 industries whose SIC definitions did not change from 1947 to 1963, thereby effectively eliminating new, rapidly growing industries.[40] Consumer and producer goods were classified according to a system used by the Federal Reserve Board. The degree of product differentiation was based on the advertising intensity of the top few firms in each industry. Industries with advertising-to-sales ratios less than 1 percent were classified as undifferentiated, those with high ratios were classified as highly differentiated, and the rest were lumped together in the middle. What exactly constituted a "high ratio" was nowhere stated explicitly. Furthermore, why advertising alone was used to classify

---

[38] Franklin R. Edwards, "Advertising and Competition in Banking," *Antitrust Bulletin*, vol. 18 (Spring 1973), pp. 23-32.

[39] Telser, "Advertising and Competition," p. 546; Robert B. Ekelund, Jr., and Charles Maurice, "An Empirical Investigation of Advertising and Concentration: Comment," *Journal of Industrial Economics*, vol. 18 (November 1969), pp. 76-80; Robert B. Ekelund, Jr., and William P. Gramm, "Advertising and Concentration: Some New Evidence," *Antitrust Bulletin*, vol. 5 (Summer 1970), pp. 243-249.

[40] Federal Trade Commission, "Comparable Concentration Ratios for 213 Manufacturing Industries Classified by Producer and Consumer Goods and Degree of Product Differentiation 1947, 1954, 1958, and 1963," March 1967.

advertising. Here we should note that these studies may be likewise biased by omitting "other" variables that affect advertising intensity. As noted above, Nelson argues that advertising intensity will vary with the informational qualities of goods, that is, whether they are search or experience goods or durable or nondurable goods. In addition, advertising intensity is commonly thought to be affected by product price, frequency of purchase, rate of new product introduction, size of market, psychological factors, and whether the goods fall into consumer or producer categories.

Previous studies have attempted to take these into account in two ways. One is by using a relatively homogeneous sample in order to reduce the importance of variables that are omitted from the regression equation. Studies attempting to explain advertising intensity generally use this approach for simplicity's sake. The other is by taking explicit account of the other factors. Studies explaining concentration have used both methods. We will look first at two studies explaining concentration using the first approach. Chapter 2 will consider studies explaining advertising intensity by the second approach.

John Vernon has attempted to explain differences in concentration ratios by costs of promotion (not merely of advertising per se) for eighteen therapeutic product classes in the ethical pharmaceutical industry.[36] In other words, Vernon studied intermarket rather than interindustry differences in concentration, while previous studies assumed in effect that industries were equivalent to economic markets. In the ethical drug industry, promotion costs include direct mail, detail men (traveling salesmen), and journal advertising. When all these were taken into account, there turned out to be no significant relationship between concentration and promotion expenditures: indeed, there was no relationship between concentration and market size, or new product sales, or market growth rate either. "There is," in Vernon's words, "no evidence that high promotion leads to high concentration within therapeutic markets. If anything, the inverse relation holds."[37] This would suggest that promotion, far from being a barrier to entry in therapeutic drugs, may instead represent a means of entry.

Franklin Edwards regressed concentration on advertising-to-sales ratios for thirty-six large banks located in twenty-three separate

---

[36] John M. Vernon, "Concentration, Promotion, and Market Share Stability in the Pharmaceutical Industry," *Journal of Industrial Economics*, vol. 19 (July 1971), pp. 246-266.

[37] Ibid., p. 259.

But if producer goods sales and advertising are included with consumer goods sales and advertising, the advertising-to-sales ratios will be distorted and subject to severe measurement error. Such errors tend to underestimate the true magnitude of a relationship and bias the correlation toward zero.[31] Finally, some IRS three-digit industries are so broad and heterogeneous as to span several economic markets.

Second, the Mann-Henning-Meehan (SIC) industries are subject to measurement and aggregation error through (1) using advertising trade sources for data that do not include all advertising and advertising-related expenditures and (2) assigning diversified firms to narrowly defined industries. Moreover, the authors used a biased sample of a few highly concentrated advertising-intensive industries: if a non-linear relationship exists, the inclusion of only high- or low-concentration industries will bias the results.[32] Telser subsequently tested the Mann-Henning-Meehan results by expanding the sample to twenty-six industries: it turned out that when the sample was broadened, the apparent relationship between advertising intensity and concentration ceased to exist.[33] These are serious statistical problems. Hence, neither original study appears to yield useful information.

Interindustry and Intermarket Studies. A number of other factors that are generally not taken into account in most interindustry studies may affect levels of industrial concentration. Advertising may, for example, be a technique for reducing the risks inherent in incorrect estimation of a firm's best (profit-maximizing) output level.[34] If risk is related to concentration, studies that do not take risk into account may be biased. It should be noted that concentration has been found to be related to certain other variables as well: economies of scale, market size, capital-intensity, and the rate of market growth.[35]

In Chapter 2, we will take up recent studies that have reversed the traditional relationship and argue that concentration explains

---

[31] Johnston, *Econometric Methods*, pp. 148-150.
[32] The average concentrations for the Mann et al. data are 60.9 (1954), 59.9 (1958), and 57.6 (1963). For Telser's observations the means are 37.7 (1947), 39.0 (1954), and 37.7 (1958). Richard A. Miller, "Advertising and Competition: Some Neglected Aspects," *Antitrust Bulletin*, vol. 17 (Summer 1972), pp. 467-478.
[33] Lester G. Telser, "Another Look at Advertising and Concentration," *Journal of Industrial Economics*, vol. 18 (November 1969), pp. 85-94.
[34] Ira Horowitz, "A Note on Advertising and Uncertainty," *Journal of Industrial Economics*, vol. 18 (November 1970), pp. 151-161.
[35] For a summary of various studies, see Stanley I. Ornstein, J. Fred Weston, Michael D. Intriligator, and Ronald E. Shrieves, "Determinants of Market Structure," *Southern Economic Journal*, vol. 39 (April 1973), pp. 612-625.

cantly associated with concentration, with intensity explaining between one-third and one-half of the variation in concentration. Since the authors assume advertising intensity is a proxy for product differentiation, they conclude that product differentiation is positively related to seller concentration.

The Mann, Henning, and Meehan study triggered a long debate focusing on statistical problems of measurement error and the interpretation of results.[29] It turns out that assigning firms to SIC industries and the IRS industries both involve severe statistical problems owing to errors in measurement and aggregating data whose net effect is indeterminate, with the measurement errors biasing correlation downward and the aggregation errors biasing it upward. Let us look briefly at the statistical problems.

First, IRS advertising and sales data come from the consolidated financial statements of firms, while the concentration ratios are based on establishment (plant) data. The IRS assigns all advertising and sales to major industry categories even though the firms are diversified, while the census data (based on what plants do rather than what firms do) avoid much of this aggregation error. Moreover, consumer and producer goods industries are subjectively defined and cannot in fact be separated using the IRS data alone, since all of a firm's output is assigned to its primary activity. (Thus, if a firm produces both "household appliances" and "electrical components and accessories," then it would be classified as producing either one category of goods or the other, but not both.) There is no way of knowing by inspection whether an IRS industry sells mostly to producers or consumers.[30]

---

[29] For the essentials, see "Symposium on Advertising and Concentration," *Journal of Industrial Economics*, vol. 18 (November 1969), pp. 76-101.

[30] An example is offered by the four industries listed below, all classified as consumer goods industries by Telser and other users of his sample. In order to determine whether the bulk of shipments went to final consumers, the percentage of output to final consumers and to producer intermediate sectors was calculated from the 1963 input-output tables. These percentages are listed next to each industry. Clearly, the majority of output in these industries did not go to final consumer demand in 1963, indicating that they were probably misclassified. On this basis other industries in the basic IRS sample used by many, such as petroleum refining and scientific instruments, also appear to be misclassified. Such errors in a small sample can obviously strongly affect the results.

		Percent of Output	
SIC	Industry	Producer intermediate goods	Consumer goods
2041	Grain mill products	72	19
2721	Periodicals	65	29
2851	Paints	94	2
3423	Hand tools	64	21

of a normal distribution is common to many statistical tests including regression and simple correlation. For an example of what a small sample can do, consider the rolling of two dice: we can predict that the two will add up to a seven six times out of thirty-six—one-sixth of the time—but that does not mean we will roll a seven one time in our first six rolls. It may take more rolls for the law of averages—sometimes called the law of large numbers—to work out. Our first six rolls might not produce a seven—the sample might be too small—but that would not mean the dice were fixed.) When correlations are calculated using the rankings of the data (to determine if the most concentrated industries had the greatest advertising intensity, the second most concentrated the second greatest intensity, and so on), it was found that there was no significant correlation.[27] This accorded with Nelson's theory.

H. M. Mann, J. A. Henning, and J. M. Meehan, Jr., argued that Telser's results suffered from measurement error, inasmuch as the Internal Revenue Service "industries" frequently do not correspond to economic markets and are composed of diversified firms, which makes it difficult to disaggregate the advertising expenditures and assign them to particular markets.[28] In an attempt to correct this error, the authors use the Department of Commerce Standard Industrial Classification (SIC) four-digit industries (the Bureau of the Census assigns SIC numbers to each establishment [plant] according to the product[s] it produces: those establishments with the same first four digits in their numbers make up a "four-digit industry"). The authors believe such industries are closer to true economic markets than three-digit IRS data compiled by firm. They regress four-firm concentration ratios on the degree of advertising intensity for forty-two firms assigned to fourteen SIC four-digit industries. Advertising intensity (measured by advertising-to-sales ratios) was calculated for the firms assigned to each industry for 1952–1956, 1957–1961, and 1962–1965. These three sets of data were correlated with concentration ratios in 1954, 1958, and 1963. Advertising intensity, in this test, was signifi-

---

[27] The simple and rank (in parentheses) correlation coefficients by experience nondurable, durable and search goods are respectively: $-.044(-.088)$, $-.213$ $(-.236)$, and $+.601(+.194)$. The correlations between advertising and profit rates are $+.780(+.767)$, $-.648(-.078)$, and $-.016(+.168)$, respectively. As seen, the significant negative profit correlation for experience durable goods is insignificant using rank correlation. Nelson explains the positive profit correlation for experience nondurable goods as spurious because the profit rate was not adjusted for the capitalized value of advertising.

[28] H. M. Mann, J. A. Henning, and J. W. Meehan, Jr., "Advertising and Concentration: An Empirical Investigation," *Journal of Industrial Economics*, vol. 16 (November 1967), pp. 34-45.

power. In fact, the R^2 (which is the measure of "explanatory power") was roughly .09 (the independent variable explained 9 percent of the variation in the dependent variable) in 1947, .10 in 1954, and .11 in 1958—data which may be roughly summarized by saying that advertising intensity is weakly related to concentration.

Telser's sample was also examined by Phillip Nelson, in accordance with Nelson's information categories, "search goods" and "experience goods" as well as durables and nodurables.[24] Nelson argues that these information categories strongly affect the extent both of advertising intensity and of concentration, so that to ignore them will falsify (bias) the conclusions one reaches. For example, Nelson's theory predicts that there will be fewer brands, and thus higher concentration, in experience goods than in search goods (holding "frequency of purchase"—durability—constant), and that there will be higher concentration in durables than in nondurables.[25] Moreover, his theory suggests that advertising-to-sales ratios will be higher for experience goods than for search goods, because a threshold level of advertising must be reached before prospective customers will sample a particular brand, and higher for nondurables than for durables because prospective purchasers of durable goods (especially expensive durables) tend to rely on guidance from nonadvertising sources such as the advice of friends and relatives.[26]

When Nelson examined Telser's data for 1958, he found no significant correlation between advertising intensity and concentration for experience nondurable and durable goods, but a significant positive correlation for search goods. Nelson allows that, although this correlation is not predicted by his theory, it may be explained by another theory: as concentration in the production of search goods rises, elasticity of demand falls, and advertising intensity rises. However, a purely statistical explanation may be appropriate. Because his samples are very small, Nelson's assumption that the distribution of the data is bivariate normal may not hold true. (The assumption

---

[24] Nelson, "The Economic Consequences of Advertising," p. 237. Darby and Karni extend Nelson's classification by arguing that in addition to experience and search qualities of goods there are credence qualities of goods. These are essentially experience qualities that cannot be evaluated in normal use without extremely high costs, for example, judging the efficacy of a prescription drug or the necessity of having an operation. In reality all goods have various degrees of and combinations of search, experience, and credence characteristics, so any distinction for empirical purposes is quite arbitrary. Michael R. Darby and Edi Karni, "Free Competition and the Optimal Amount of Fraud," *Journal of Law and Economics*, vol. 16 (April 1973), pp. 67-88.

[25] Nelson, "Information and Consumer Behavior," p. 320.

[26] Nelson, "Advertising as Information," pp. 738, 747.

Figure 1
HYPOTHETICAL ADVERTISING / CONCENTRATION RELATIONSHIP

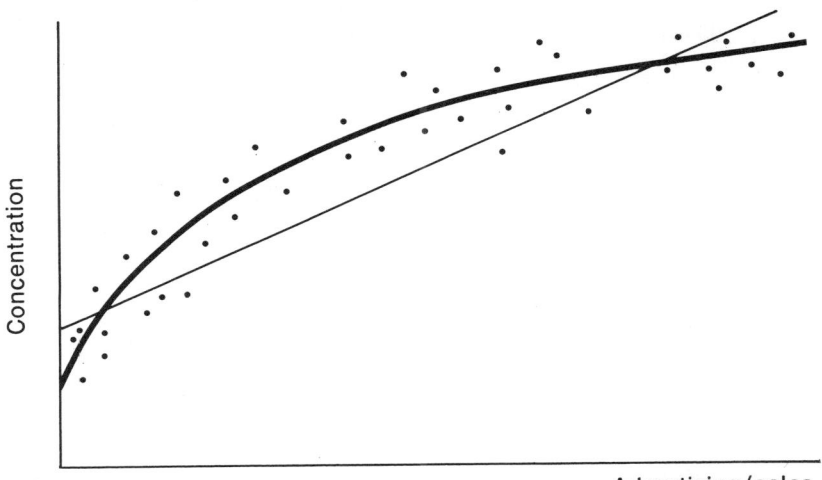

or increasing rate. Correspondingly, our observations would support the hypothesis that there exists a nonlinear, but still a significant and positive relationship, between advertising and concentration. Suppose each dot in Figure 1 matches an observed level of concentration with an observed level of advertising intensity. The true relationship between concentration and advertising intensity is represented by the nonlinear, bold line, while the straight, thin line is seen to fit the data poorly.

This particular problem can be handled in various ways, but the most common is to look for a straight-line relationship among the logarithms of the variables.[22] David Kamerschen found statistically significant relationships among the logarithms of Telser's variables in each of the three years.[23] However, even these relationships, albeit statistically significant, were not remarkable for their explanatory

---

[22] The basic model Telser tested was $CR = a + b(A/S) + u$, where CR = four-firm concentration ratio, (A/S) = advertising-sales ratio, and u = error term. Alternatively, the variables may be related nonlinearly in the multiplicative form, $CR = a(A/S)^b u$. This can be transformed into a linear expression by taking logs of each side, yielding $\text{Log}CR = \text{Log}a + \text{Log}b(A/S) + \text{Log}u$. For a description of least squares estimation see a standard econometric text, such as J. Johnston, *Econometric Methods* (New York: McGraw-Hill, 1963), or Ronald J. Wonnacott and Thomas H. Wonnacott, *Econometrics* (New York: John Wiley and Sons, 1970).

[23] David R. Kamerschen, "The Statistics of Advertising," *Rivista Internazionale di Scienze Economiche e Commerciali*, vol. 19 (January 1972), pp. 1-25.

for the 80 percent. Kaldor and Silverman interpreted this finding as suggesting an inverted-U or quadratic relationship, with advertising intensity and concentration positively related up to some intermediate concentration level and negatively (inversely) related thereafter. They concluded that large-scale advertising is unique to oligopolistic industries (those where four to nine firms account for more than 80 percent of the advertising), with small-scale advertising characteristic of monopolies and of competitive industries.

In his re-examination of the Kaldor-Silverman results, Morton Schnabel suggested that the use of average advertising-to-sales ratios to measure advertising intensity was suspect.[19] First, there was considerable variance in the ratios, and second, Kaldor and Silverman had imputed ratios to individual commodities on the basis of the ratios for groups of commodities. This introduced a bias into the results. When the results were corrected for the bias induced by the method of imputation, Schnabel found that the so-called oligopolistic range ran not from four to nine but from two to twenty-one firms (almost the whole range of the original sample), a fact which would seem to cast considerable doubt on the Kaldor-Silverman findings.

Lester Telser was the first to carry out statistical tests for a linear or straight-line relationship between advertising and industrial concentration.[20] He regressed concentration on advertising intensity in 1947, 1954, and 1958 for forty-two Internal Revenue Service industries classified by Telser as consumer goods industries. The results show no significant positive correlation between the two variables: advertising variations explained less than 3 percent of the concentration variations.[21] Changes in advertising and changes in concentration between the various pairs of years—1947–1958, 1947–1954, and 1954–1958—were also insignificant with even lower correlation.

Telser's hypothesis that a linear relationship exists between advertising and concentration could have been wrong even though a significant positive relationship did exist. For example, we might observe that advertising intensity rises with concentration, not at a constant rate, as a linear relationship would imply, but at a decreasing

---

[19] Morton Schnabel, "A Note on Advertising and Industrial Concentration," *Journal of Political Economy*, vol. 78 (September/October 1970), pp. 1191-1194.
[20] Telser, "Advertising and Competition," pp. 537-562.
[21] To speak of one or a group of variables "explaining" another is a statistical expression meaning that the regression line is fitted to the data in such a way as to "explain" some percentage of the variation in the dependent variable. In order to predict future values of the dependent variable, the goal is naturally to explain as much of the variation as possible. However, this says nothing about causation. The statistical term for percentage of explained variation is the coefficient of determination, symbolized as R^2.

13

doubtful. Jean-Jacques Lambin found that buyer inertia (his empirical equivalent of loyalty) is strongly influenced by product performance and quality and little influenced by advertising.[14] He argues that advertising cannot artificially create brand loyalty. After more than twenty years of research on brand loyalty by marketing experts, there is no evidence that brand loyalty is related to advertising.[15] Indeed, there is evidence that price and advertising elasticity do not differ among brand loyal and nonloyal shoppers.[16] It appears there is little, if any, empirical basis for the Kaldor-Bain proposition that advertising creates brand loyalty.

Based on studies of brand loyalty, it may be hypothesized that advertising is used to establish initial buyer-seller contact and to reinforce initial purchases but that product characteristics, price, habit, and consumer experience dictate subsequent purchase. No amount of advertising can overcome the attributes of a bad product. Alternatively, advertising may lead to disloyalty by bringing new products to the attention of consumers. In support of this view, there is strong empirical evidence showing that market shares are more unstable in advertising-intensive markets than in low-advertising markets and that rival firms' advertising has a significant negative effect on a firm's market share.[17]

Tests on Advertising and Concentration. The first test for a relationship between advertising and concentration was made by Kaldor and Silverman in the 1940s on data from 1938.[18] For 118 commodities in Great Britain, they examined advertising intensity and advertising concentration, which is measured according to the number of firms needed to account for 80 percent of industry advertising expenditures in the press. Advertising intensity turned out to be highest for the eight-firm advertising concentration level, declining substantially when four or fewer firms or nine or more firms were needed to account

---

[14] Lambin, *Advertising, Competition, and Market Conduct*, pp. 117-118.
[15] James F. Engel, David T. Kollat, and Roger D. Blackwell, *Consumer Behavior*, 2nd ed. (Hinsdale, Ill.: Dryden Press, 1973), chapter 23.
[16] William F. Massy and Ronald E. Frank, "Short-Term Price and Demand Effects in Selected Market Segments," *Journal of Marketing Research*, vol. 2 (May 1965), pp. 171-185.
[17] Lester G. Telser, "Advertising and Competition," *Journal of Political Economy*, vol. 72 (December 1964), pp. 537-562; W. Duncan Reekie, "Advertising and Market Share Mobility," *Scottish Journal of Political Economy*, vol. 21 (June 1974), pp. 143-158; Lambin, *Advertising, Competition, and Market Conduct*, p. 107.
[18] Nicholas Kaldor and Rodney Silverman, *A Statistical Analysis of Advertising Expenditure and Revenue of the Press* (Cambridge: Cambridge University Press, 1948).

studies and cross-sectional analyses of increasing returns to advertising.[11] They unanimously conclude that there is no evidence whatever of scale economies in advertising. There is, for example, no evidence of quantity discounts or price discrimination in favor of large-scale television advertisers.[12] Nor is there evidence of increasing advertising effectiveness attributable to increasing frequency of advertising messages or audience size—indeed, most studies find evidence of decreasing returns to advertising.[13] In short, there seems to be no evidence that scale economies in advertising exist and, therefore, that scale economies can lead to increased concentration.

Although no tests have been made on the capital barriers to entry that are supposed to result from economies of scale and brand loyalty, logic suggests that such barriers would be rare even if scale economies did exist and advertising caused brand loyalty. First, there is a large pool of potential entrants in other industries whose costs of capital are as low as, or lower than, the costs of the existing firms in the industry they may wish to enter. As for any excess profits that might be reaped by a potential entrant, there is an efficiently functioning capital market ready to supply funds for that entrant—whether the funds are venture capital for new entrants or debt and equity capital for well-established giants. Second, advertising is not indivisible, requiring only large outlays. Each advertising medium offers a range of advertising time or space and can provide services directed at local, regional, or national markets or at combinations of local and regional markets.

The evidence on brand loyalty and advertising suggests that advertising is not a strong determinant of brand loyalty. Brand loyalty certainly exists (although there is confusion as to just how to measure it), but whether it is caused or can be influenced by advertising is

---

[11] Julian L. Simon, *Issues in the Economics of Advertising* (Urbana: University of Illinois Press, 1970); Richard Schmalensee, *The Economics of Advertising* (Amsterdam: North-Holland, 1972); Ferguson, *Advertising and Competition*.

[12] John L. Peterman, "The Structure of National Time Rates in the Television Broadcasting Industry," *Journal of Law and Economics*, vol. 8 (October 1965), pp. 77-132, and David Blank, "Television Advertising: The Great Discount Illusion, or Tonypandy Revisited," *Journal of Business*, vol. 41 (January 1968), pp. 10-38. These studies show that discounts in television advertising are a method of equalizing cost per message delivered and that they do not result in economies for large advertisers.

[13] See Jean-Jacques Lambin, *Advertising, Competition, and Market Conduct in Oligopoly over Time: An Econometric Investigation in Western European Countries* (Amsterdam: North-Holland, 1976), pp. 95-98; the main results are summarized in "What Is the Real Impact of Advertising?" *Harvard Business Review*, vol. 53 (May/June 1975), pp. 139-147.

past or present sales. This suggests that advertising and concentration are inversely related.

On the other hand, Nelson argues that, before advertising or without it, the largest firms will be most efficient, having the ability to produce their goods at lower prices per unit of utility than the smaller, less efficient firms can.[10] Since the gains to advertising are greater for the most efficient firms (that is, the ones offering advertised goods at the lowest prices per unit of utility), those firms have the greatest incentive to advertise. Thus, the largest firms will prosper at the expense of the smaller, less efficient firms, and advertising will increase concentration. Nelson concludes that these effects are counterbalancing and that there is no way to tell which of the two is the stronger.

The difference between the Kaldor-Bain-Comanor-Wilson model and the Nelson model comes down to the effect of advertising on brand loyalty and economies of scale on the one hand and the effectiveness of advertising in providing information and reducing search costs on the other. One theory postulates that advertising changes consumer tastes, reduces price elasticity, and increases monopoly power, and the other theory postulates that advertising increases information, increases price elasticity, and reduces monopoly power. To gain some perspective on where the truth may lie, let us look now at some of the tests that have been carried out on the extent of advertising scale economies, advertising-induced brand loyalty, and the relationship between advertising and concentration.

Empirical Tests

Empirical tests of the hypothesis that advertising causes increased concentration fall generally into two categories: (1) direct tests for a positive correlation between advertising intensity and concentration ratios, and (2) tests for economies of scale in advertising (increasing returns per dollar as advertising expenditures increase) and for capital barriers to entry. We will begin with tests for economies of scale.

Tests for Economics of Scale and Brand Loyalty. Simon, Schmalensee, and Ferguson have reviewed the literature on time-series demand

---

[10] Nelson defines price in this way to standardize it by a unit of utility or, in crude terms, consumer satisfaction. Alternatively, one can think of a price per unit of quality. Both concepts are ambiguous empirically since measures of utility or quality do not exist. However, the notion of quality seems to have a clearer connotation to most people than utility.

tion and tests deductions drawn from this analysis against data from the market. He defines monopoly power as the difference between price and marginal cost and analyzes the relationship between advertising and monopoly power. His model shows that advertising reduces monopoly power by increasing price elasticity and facilitating entry. In his model, Nelson divides consumer goods into "search" and "experience" categories. Those goods whose main characteristics can be determined prior to purchase, such as the style of an article of clothing, are defined as "search" goods. Those goods whose main characteristics can be determined only by use and experience, such as the taste of a can of food, are defined as "experience" goods. Both the nature and the costs of consumer search differ according to the nature of the good in question, and the difference affects the amounts that will be spent on advertising.

Nelson's model starts with extremely simplified assumptions. He begins by assuming that every consumer is like every other consumer—all have the same sets of preferences with the same values attached to each (that is, the same "utility functions") and face the same costs of search. In this model, it is lack of information on product substitutes that is a chief cause of price-inelastic demand. The rate of demand becomes more responsive to changes in price because advertising increases the amount of information available on product substitutes. Since the increased price-elasticity of demand leads to reduced prices (through price competition) it follows that advertising reduces the difference between price and marginal cost and therefore reduces monopoly power.

The effects of advertising on concentration (as opposed to monopoly power per se) are ambiguous. On the one hand, according to Nelson, entry is generally easier in a market with advertising than in a market without advertising. In a market without advertising, consumers must rely on such nonrandom sampling procedures as asking advice from friends and relatives, reading consumer magazines, and observing brands in use. Where advertising is present, it will be used along with these information sources by some consumers, thus increasing the probability that they will sample a new brand. This is especially true inasmuch as advice from friends and relatives and observations of brands already on the market provide little information on new market entries, while advertising based on future expected sales can be used to promote new as well as old brands. Hence, a new entrant can capture a share of the market where consumers are guided by advertising in contrast to information based on

barriers to entry by new firms because of the capital needed to overcome brand loyalty and to realize economies of scale.[7] Unlike Bain, they have argued that economies of scale in advertising are substantial owing to quantity discounts in the advertising media and to the increasing effectiveness of advertising once it reaches the threshold level required for it to be competitive. Economies of scale are regarded as a barrier to entry whenever optimum firm size is large relative to the size of market, inasmuch as the entry of new firms will decrease prices for all firms—new and old—and perhaps shift demand below cost, imposing losses on all firms. Like Bain, Comanor and Wilson also argued that with imperfect capital markets, entrants will face high capital barriers to entry. Inasmuch as concentration ratios are a priori related to nonlegal barriers to entry, especially barriers attributable to economies of scale, then advertising is a strong candidate for explaining concentration ratios in consumer goods industries.[8]

The view that advertising is the main basis for product differentiation and brand loyalty and is a barrier to entry is well entrenched and has rarely been challenged. The argument running from Kaldor through Bain to Comanor and Wilson echoes this view, though with differing emphasis. Implicit or explicit in this argument is the assumption that advertising changes consumer tastes or, at the very least, reinforces existing tastes to the point where they will be extremely difficult to change. In a recent series of articles, Phillip Nelson has rejected this assumption, and it is instructive to see where that has led him.[9]

Arguing that there is no economic theory of consumer tastes yielding testable deductions, Nelson analyzes advertising as informa-

---

[7] William S. Comanor and Thomas A. Wilson, "Advertising, Market Structure and Performance," *Review of Economics and Statistics*, vol. 49 (November 1967), pp. 423-440.

[8] In fairness to Comanor and Wilson, it should be pointed out that based on simple correlation analysis they found that advertising intensity and concentration are independent. However, this is contradicted by both their theory and their evidence, which imply a positive relationship. Their empirical results show that economies of scale and capital barriers to entry at the plant level, holding regional industry differences constant, explain 81 percent of the variation in concentration ratios across their sample of consumer goods industries. Since the major part of their theory is devoted to arguing that advertising leads to economies of scale and capital barriers to entry, it follows from this result that advertising must be correlated with concentration.

[9] Phillip Nelson, "Information and Consumer Behavior," *Journal of Political Economy*, vol. 78 (March/April 1970), pp. 311-329; "Advertising as Information," *Journal of Political Economy*, vol. 81 (July/August 1974), pp. 729-754; "The Economic Consequences of Advertising," *Journal of Business*, vol. 48 (April 1975), pp. 213-241.

advertising, although later economists stressed only his argument that advertising leads to greater concentration.

Most empirical studies of the relationship between advertising and industrial concentration using U.S. data turn to Joe Bain's work on barriers to entry as the theoretical basis for a positive relationship.[3] Bain argued that strong product differentiation and brand loyalty are frequently the basis for high concentration and barriers to entry in consumer goods industries (which is Kaldor's argument also). He went on to postulate a general tendency for buyers to prefer established products to new products. This tendency places new entrants into a market at a cost disadvantage stemming from capital market constraints and possible economies of scale in advertising. To compete, new entrants must have access to enough capital either to outspend their established rivals on advertising or to sell below existing prices for considerable periods of time. Although Bain was ambivalent about the extent of economies of scale for advertising in the national media, he firmly held that new entrants would incur higher costs of capital and enjoy less access to capital than established firms.[4]

Bain argued that advertising plays a significant role in product differentiation but that product differentiation and brand loyalty depend also on such other factors as product durability and complexity, frequency of purchase, consumer knowledge, and motives connected with what Thorstein Veblen called "conspicuous consumption" (consumption as a way to boast of one's wealth). These other factors, Bain concluded, "may also suggest that advertising per se is not necessarily the main or most important key to the product differentiation problem as it affects intraindustry competition and the condition of entry."[5] Students of Bain who have used advertising as the main proxy for product differentiation may therefore have misinterpreted him.[6] More to our point, it would appear that Bain's argument is for the most part Kaldor's argument, expanded and somewhat qualified.

William Comanor and Thomas Wilson have expanded the argument that advertising expenditures by existing firms raise capital

---

[3] Joe S. Bain, *Barriers to New Competition* (Cambridge, Mass.: Harvard University Press, 1956).
[4] Ibid., pp. 65-67, 141.
[5] Ibid., p. 143.
[6] Bain does classify the cigarette industry as having high product differentiation barriers to entry solely on the basis of its advertising. Brand loyalty based on advertising was also an important reason for high product differentiation barriers to entry in typewriters, liquor, high-quality fountain pens, and automobiles, according to Bain. Ibid., p. 129.

On the question narrowly defined, Kaldor argued that the "real secret" of advertising lay in its effect on the market shares held by different firms within an industry. The introduction of advertising into an industry would eventually increase concentration for two reasons. First, the larger a firm's expenditures on advertising, the greater the "pulling power" of the advertising (the sales responsiveness per advertising dollar)—that is to say, there are increasing returns to scale in advertising. Second, firms that are successful in advertising will increase their market share still further by reinvesting their profits in still more advertising. Kaldor explicitly assumed that a firm's advertising expenditures are in proportion to its sales and implicitly assumed that imperfect capital markets make it impossible for small firms to match the advertising expenditures of large firms. Returns to advertising do not, however (according to his argument), increase indefinitely but eventually level off and then begin to diminish, limiting the concentration induced by advertising to the oligopoly level. Also, he believed the process to be reversible, so that decreased advertising expenditures would lead to reduced concentration.

Kaldor asked not whether advertising caused resources to be misallocated by its mere existence but whether it did so by increasing concentration, thereby reducing the competitiveness of markets. Is the high concentration that is brought about by advertising necessary for technological advance and economies of scale in production? If so, are these gains more than offset by welfare losses attributable to the resource misallocation created by oligopolistic collusion?

Besides this, Kaldor argued that advertising "differentiates" goods, creating brand loyalty and reducing the effectiveness of price competition. Since overcoming this brand loyalty is expensive, the advertising that created the brand loyalty also created high capital barriers to market entry. Kaldor also held that price competition is nearly nonexistent in oligopolies, while advertising and other selling expenses are high—thus holding, in effect, that market concentration creates increased advertising intensity. Kaldor was one of the first to recognize the potential interacting effects of concentration and

---

in the 1880s and 1890s did not destroy an atomistic market system, but transformed local and regional oligopolies to national oligopolies, if the southern experience can be extended to the rest of the nation. Fred Bateman and Thomas Weiss, "Market Structure before the Age of Big Business: Concentration and Profit in Early Southern Manufacturing," *Business History Review*, vol. 44 (Autumn 1975), pp. 312-336; Ambrose P. Winston, "The Chimera of Monopoly," *Atlantic Monthly*, vol. 134 (November 1924), pp. 681-692, reprinted in *The Freeman*, September 1960, pp. 39-52.

1
DOES ADVERTISING CAUSE INCREASED CONCENTRATION?

Theoretical Background

Some twenty-five years ago the Cambridge (England) economist Nicholas Kaldor outlined the argument that advertising causes increased industrial concentration.[1] The position taken in his article has dominated academic thinking ever since. It is important to note, however, that Kaldor's paper defines the question of increased industrial concentration both broadly and narrowly, that his argument on the question broadly defined is essentially historical and his argument on the question narrowly defined essentially theoretical.

On the question broadly defined, Kaldor maintained that advertising in late nineteenth century England increased concentration by transforming the overall market structure so that national (noncompetitive) oligopolies replaced many local and regional competitors. Before the rise of large-scale advertising, in his view, the distribution of goods in England rested with a small group of wholesalers who were supplied by numerous small, independent, competitive firms. But in the late nineteenth century the manufacturers, desirous of transferring loyalty to themselves, began to advertise heavily, thus developing brand loyalty and customer good will for their products. The result was product standardization, longer production runs, economies of scale—and thus increased concentration.[2]

---

[1] Nicholas Kaldor, "The Economic Aspects of Advertising," *Review of Economic Studies*, vol. 18 (1949-1950), pp. 1-27.

[2] The view expounded by most economists and historians is that prior to the great merger wave around 1900, the U.S. economy consisted of numerous, local unconcentrated markets. Recent evidence, however, shows otherwise. In the antebellum South of 1850-1860, manufacturing concentration was quite high on both a state and a regional basis. It appears that the rise of national oligopolies

as an index of monopoly power.³ Specifically, monopoly power has been attributed to the concentration of output in the largest firms in an industry. As a result, economists trying to determine whether advertising decreases competition have tested for a positive statistical relationship between advertising intensity (generally the advertising-to-sales ratio) and industrial concentration and have drawn inferences about the effects of advertising via concentration on the degree of competition in various industries.⁴ This procedure is subject to some difficulties—one, in general, being that statistical relationships do not demonstrate causality, and another (or rather a set of others) lying in the errors to which the statistical procedures themselves are subject. The more pronounced these difficulties in the statistics, the less reliable the inferences that may be drawn from them. If the literature that tests for a positive relationship between advertising intensity and industrial concentration appears confused, so also, it would seem, are any public policies that may be based on this literature.

Accordingly, Chapter 1 of the study reviews past theoretical and empirical work generally used to support the contention that advertising increases industrial concentration, while Chapter 2 reviews the work generally used to support the opposite contention, that industrial concentration increases advertising intensity. Chapter 3 presents some alternative hypotheses and new findings based on new data. The policy implications of the past studies and the new findings are summarized in Chapter 4.

---

³ For a contrary view, see Demsetz, *Market Concentration Doctrine*. Also, Office of Policy Planning and Evaluation, *1976 Budget Overview of the Federal Trade Commission*; Bureau of National Affairs, Antitrust Trade Regulation Report E-1, December 10, 1974; and McGee, *In Defense of Industrial Concentration*.

⁴ Another group of studies has tested for a positive relationship between advertising intensity and profit rates with the latter variable assumed to be a proxy for monopoly power. For a review of these studies, see James M. Ferguson, *Advertising and Competition: Theory, Measurement, Fact* (Cambridge, Mass.: Ballinger, 1975).

to entry, advertising facilitates entry by allowing previously unknown products to gain rapid market acceptance. Without advertising, market penetration would be much slower for new products than it is with advertising. Advertising serves consumers by increasing product variety and by permitting firms to exploit economies of scale in production and distribution—which in turn yields lower consumer prices.

To say that these two views are divergent is to understate the case. In one view advertising is an integral part of the competitive process, leading to increased consumer welfare. In the other view, advertising is a key element in constructing a monopoly, to the detriment of society. The Federal Trade Commission has recently come down firmly on both sides of the issue. The "advertising creates monopoly" view (or at least the view that advertising and monopoly go hand in hand) is the basis for the FTC case against the four leading producers of breakfast cereals.[1] The FTC has charged that these companies maintain a shared monopoly in part through excessive expenditures on advertising, which insulates the companies from competition by new entrants into the market, producing collusive behavior and the exercise of monopoly power. On the other hand, the "advertising is competitive" view is the basis for the proposed FTC trade regulation rule that would revoke the ban on the advertising of prescription eyeglasses—a ban now imposed by several states.[2] Proponents of this rule hold that the ban restricts consumer information, restricts price competition, and increases search costs to the consumer. The apparent inconsistency in these two actions is clear. If advertising leads to high concentration and high barriers to entry, as argued in the cereals case, will it not transform the eyeglass industry within each state into a similar market structure? The FTC's simultaneous support of these divergent views on advertising reflects the influence of economic theories on government actions. The question is, "Which theory is correct?"

The purpose of this study is to examine the relationship between advertising and market structure (the degree of industrial concentration) in order to see whether that relationship can reasonably be used as the basis for public policy. The reason for the focus on market structure lies in its wide—but certainly not total—acceptance

---

[1] Kellogg Company, General Mills, Inc., General Foods Corporation, the Quaker Oats Company Complaint, Docket No. 8883, Federal Trade Commission, April 26, 1972.
[2] "Advertising of Ophthalmic Goods and Services," *Federal Register*, vol. 41 (January 16, 1976), p. 2399.

though in fact it has never been rigorously set down. Advertising supposedly leads to strong brand loyalty among buyers of an advertised product. Demand for this product then becomes less price-elastic than it was before—that is, demand is determined by brand loyalty and is relatively insensitive to price (consumers will buy, say, Bayer Aspirin at double the price of other aspirin because to them "aspirin" means "Bayer")—and price rises above competitive levels. Entry of new producers into the field, or effective competition by existing producers, is impeded because of the high advertising costs that would have to be incurred to overcome this brand loyalty. Connected with this part of the argument is the view that there are economies of (or increasing returns to) scale in advertising (that is, the view that the more a firm spends for advertising, the greater is the return for each additional dollar spent).

These presumed economies of scale will increase the advantages of large firms over small firms and of old firms over new firms. Economies of scale in advertising for established firms are reinforced by the superior access to capital markets that is supposedly enjoyed by large old firms. Successful advertisers will grow at the expense of their rivals, even though their growth may in fact take them beyond the firm size that would be best from the viewpoint of economic efficiency—or even though (as an alternative) the growth induced by advertising may lead to a larger optimum size that will make it even harder for rivals to compete. In short, advertising increases industrial concentration (defined as the share of an industry's market held by the few largest firms in the industry), raises barriers to entry, and therefore leads to collusion and the exercise of monopoly power. The result is restricted output, raised prices, inefficient allocation of resources, long-run excess profits for the monopolists, and distortion in the distribution of wealth.

In recent years the traditional view has been challenged by an alternative view which concludes that advertising improves the allocation of resources. The essence of this new view is that advertising provides information on brands, prices, and quality, thus increasing buyer knowledge, reducing consumers' search costs, and reducing the total costs to society of transacting business. Advertising induces sellers to improve the quality of goods: better informed buyers are not likely to purchase or repurchase low-quality or unsatisfactory goods. By increasing information, advertising increases the number of substitutes known to buyers, thereby increasing the price elasticity of demand and reducing price-cost margins. Far from being a barrier

INTRODUCTION

The influence of economists' ideas on government actions is the subject of much debate. Some believe that the power of ideas determines governmental decisions; others believe the government is run not by wisdom but by vanity. In those matters which are the subject of this study the ideas of economists appear to have a grip on political and bureaucratic attitudes: opponents of advertising who see dishonesty, manipulation of consumer preferences, and the creation of "false" values based on materialism in most commercial messages have—until recently, at least—ordinarily found comfort in the writing of economists. Because of the apparent influence of economists, much of what follows is a discussion of the economic literature on advertising, a part of which has become the basis for some recent governmental antitrust actions.

While economists have contributed to debates on the above issues, they have been concerned primarily with the "efficiency" aspects of advertising. Is advertising a source of competition or of monopoly? Does advertising improve the allocation of resources in a market or lead to a misallocation of resources? More particularly, is there a necessary connection between advertising and industrial concentration (with industrial concentration being taken for the moment as a proxy for monopoly power)? The traditional view, in general, is that there is a necessary and positive connection, though there is some doubt which is cause and which effect. A newer view is that advertising is positively related not to monopoly but to competition. The purpose of this paper is not to prove the truth of the second view but to examine the theoretical and factual basis for the first. If that basis is weak, then presumably the antitrust opponents of advertising must look elsewhere for a scientific defense of their attitudes and policies.

The argument for the traditional view may be briefly summarized, are aimed at deconcentrating the industrial system. But if the alleged dangers of industrial concentration are farfetched, then all the more farfetched are worries about an insidious, symbiotic relationship between industrial concentration and advertising. If concentration does not directly threaten performance, then advertising can hardly threaten performance indirectly by "causing" concentration.

The study that follows would be of value even if a few economists' worries about advertising and concentration had not escalated, as they have, into litigation that aims to break up (or in some other way penalize) large advertisers simply for being large: it is occasionally worthwhile to ask whether a particular line of scientific inquiry appears to be leading anywhere. As it turns out, however, the advertising-concentration controversy is no longer a merely academic matter. The idea has taken hold that advertising is a predatory tactic used by some firms to grow large and strong at the expense of rivals. Thus, a Federal Trade Commission judge has ruled Borden, Inc., in violation of the FTC Act in part by virtue of promotional methods that allegedly brought about the "dominance" of its ReaLemon brand over the brands sold by other makers of reconstituted lemon juice.[2] One soup company has charged another with "predatory advertising," leading to monopoly,[3] and the FTC presses its complaint against the major cereals makers for using advertising to maintain a "shared monopoly."[4]

Although Ornstein advises against such actions, his message is not merely negative. Using input-output and census data, he shows how empirical research may yield a number of interesting insights on industrial phenomena, provided the inferences are cautiously drawn. However, the urgency of his study lies in the speed with which both scholars and policy makers appear to be jumping to conclusions about the advertising-concentration relationship, unmindful of just how complex that relationship really is.

DAVID G. TUERCK
Center for Research on Advertising
American Enterprise Institute

[2] Borden, Inc., Case, Docket No. 8978, Federal Trade Commission, August 1976, p. 67.
[3] H. J. Heinz Company v. Campbell Soup Company, Civil Action No. 76-1306 (W.D. Pa. 1976), p. 10 of plaintiff's complaint. In another example, one conglomerate is being threatened with litigation for allegedly using the profits generated by one of its subsidiaries to underwrite the promotional efforts of another. See "Miller's Fast Growth Upsets the Beer Industry," *Business Week*, November 8, 1976, p. 61.
[4] Kellogg Company, General Mills, Inc., General Foods Corporation, The Quaker Oats Company Complaint, Docket No. 8883, Federal Trade Commission, April 1972, pp. 7, 8, 9.

FOREWORD

It is an interesting question how economists come to allocate their time among the various public policy issues that compete for it. Some issues—inflation, unemployment, energy, the environment—seem to deserve the attention they get. Others, such as the one that Stanley Ornstein examines below, seem to have been blown far out of proportion to their importance. What Dr. Ornstein provides is not only an exhaustive review and evaluation of an issue that has—however curiously—come to loom large in discussions of industrial organization but also a warning against combining bad statistics with bad theory. In this case, the statistics measure phenomena—industrial "concentration" and advertising "intensity"—that supposedly interact in some way that threatens consumer welfare.

Empirical research, even when carefully done, can confuse public policy when the theory tested by it is poorly understood in the first place. Such research invites careless readers to draw sweeping inferences that support preconceived notions of how measured phenomena interrelate. Other and equally plausible inferences may be ignored to the detriment of both science and policy. As Ornstein explains, for example, an observed positive relationship between industrial concentration and advertising intensity is consistent with the theory that concentration "causes" advertising as well as the theory that advertising "causes" concentration. Yet, the second interpretation appears to be increasingly preferred in antitrust complaints.

The argument that industrial concentration poses a threat to consumer welfare is itself disputable.[1] Studies that examine critically the relevant economic literature argue against antitrust policies that

---

[1] See, for example, Harold Demsetz, *The Market Concentration Doctrine* (Washington, D.C.: American Enterprise Institute, 1973), and John S. McGee, *In Defense of Industrial Concentration* (New York: Praeger, 1971).

CONTENTS

FOREWORD

INTRODUCTION   1

1 DOES ADVERTISING CAUSE INCREASED CONCENTRATION?   5

    Theoretical Background   5
    Empirical Tests   10
    Summary   23

2 DOES CONCENTRATION CAUSE INCREASED ADVERTISING?   25

    Advertising and the Behavior of Oligopolies   26
    Review of Major Studies   29
    Summary   37

3 NEW FINDINGS   39

    New Models   42
    The Results   46
    Summary   62

4 CONCLUSION   63

APPENDIX   67

Stanley I. Ornstein is assistant research economist at the Graduate School of Management, University of California, Los Angeles.

Portions of this study were excerpted from Stanley I. Ornstein, "The Advertising-Concentration Controversy," *Southern Economic Journal*, vol. 43 (July 1976), with permission.

Library of Congress Cataloging in Publication Data

Ornstein, Stanley I
    Industrial concentration and advertising intensity.

    (AEI studies; 152)
    1. Advertising. 2. Industrial concentration.
I. Title. II. Series: American Enterprise Institute for Public Policy Research. AEI studies ; 152.
HF5827.076   338'.09   77-5776
ISBN 0-8447-3250-8

AEI studies 152

© 1977 by American Enterprise Institute for Public Policy Research, Washington, D.C. Permission to quote from or to reproduce materials in this publication is granted when due acknowledgment is made.

Printed in the United States of America

Industrial Concentration and Advertising Intensity

Stanley I. Ornstein

American Enterprise Institute for Public Policy Research
Washington, D.C.

Industrial Concentration and Advertising Intensity